A Sense of Wonder

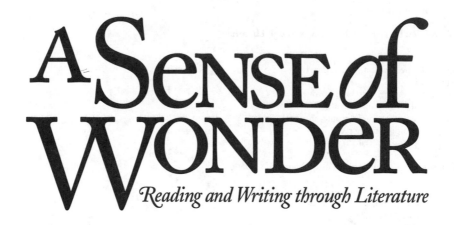

A Sense of Wonder

Reading and Writing through Literature

BILL PRESTON

Longman

longman.com

For all my teachers and students

A Sense of Wonder: Reading and Writing through Literature

Copyright © 2003 by Pearson Education, Inc.
All rights reserved.
No part of this publication may be reproduced,
stored in a retrieval system, or transmitted
in any form or by any means, electronic, mechanical,
photocopying, recording, or otherwise,
without the prior permission of the publisher.

Pearson Education, 10 Bank Street, White Plains, NY 10606

Vice president, director of instructional design: Allen Ascher
Senior acquisitions editor: Laura Le Dréan
Development director: Penny Laporte
Development editor: Paula H. Van Ells
Vice president, director of design and production: Rhea Banker
Director of electronic production: Aliza Greenblatt
Executive managing editor: Linda Moser
Production manager: Ray Keating
Associate production editor: Michael Goldberg
Director of manufacturing: Patrice Fraccio
Senior manufacturing buyer: Dave Dickey
Photo research: Mykan White
Cover and text design: Debbie Iverson
Text composition: Lisa Ghiozzi
Text font: ACaslon, Gill Sans
Illustrations: Ronald Chironna
Text credits: See page xv.
Photo credits: See page xvi.

Longman wishes to thank the reviewers of *A Sense of Wonder:*
Lynn Bonesteel, Boston University, Boston, MA
Linda Fellag, Community College of Philadelphia, Philadelphia, PA
Carole Franklin, University of Houston, Houston, TX
Kathy Hitchcox, California State University, Fresno, CA
John Milbury-Steen, Temple University, Philadelphia, PA
Caitlin Morgan, Hunter College, New York, NY
Herbert Pierson, St. John's University, Jamaica, NY
Marc Roberts, Pine Manor College, Chestnut Hill, MA
Barbara Smith-Palinkas, University of South Florida, Tampa, FL

Library of Congress Cataloging-in-Publication Data

A sense of wonder: reading and writing through literature / Bill Preston.
        p. cm.
    ISBN 0-13-040560-4
    1. Readers--Minorities.   2. English language--Textbooks for foreign speakers.
3. English language--Rhetoric--Problems, exercises, etc.   4. Report writing--
Problems, exercises, etc.   5. American literature--Minority authors.   6. Minorities--
Literary collections.   I. Preston, Bill.

PE1127.M5 S46 2002
808'.0427--dc21

                                                                    2002022244

Printed in the United States of America
1 2 3 4 5 6 7 8 9 10–VHG–07 06 05 04 03 02

Contents

Scope and Sequence

GENRE	READING FOCUS	LITERATURE FOCUS
poem	Visualizing	Poetic License; Alliteration
essay	Sequence Words	Similes
poem	—	Metaphors
story	Guessing Meaning from Context	Onomatopoeia
poem	Pronoun Referents	Sensory Images
story	Quoted and Reported Speech	Verbal Irony
poem	Making Prose Sense of a Poem	Personification
story	Making Inferences	Similes and Metaphors
poem	A Moral	An Ode
essay	Making Inferences	Thesis and Antithesis
poem	Making Inferences	Figures of Speech
play	Reduced Forms	Backstory
poem	Making Inferences	Literal and Figurative Meanings
essay	Guessing Meaning from Context	Theme and Thesis
story	Distinguishing Fact from Opinion	Hyperbole
poem	Visualizing	Fantasy
poem	Pronoun Referents	Dramatic Monologue
play	Reduced Forms	Characterization
story	Inferring a Moral	Dramatic Irony
essay	Theme	Motif
story	Making Predictions	Conflict
essay	Phrasal Verbs	Flashbacks
story	Register	Mood
poem	—	List Poem; Chant

To the Teacher

A Sense of Wonder is an anthology of literature for secondary, young adult, and adult students studying English as a second or foreign language. It includes authentic poetry, essays, plays, and short stories, whose writers represent a diversity of cultures, backgrounds, and points of view.

In addition to providing students with skills for understanding and appreciating literature, the reading and writing components of *A Sense of Wonder* complement and reinforce each other by giving students integrated practice in key language skills.

As a reading text, *A Sense of Wonder* offers multiple activities for students to access background knowledge of the themes and ideas presented in the literary pieces, and poses questions for them to consider as they read. In post-reading activities, students check comprehension of main ideas, and discuss and interpret the more subtle points of the selections. In special Focus on Reading and Focus on Literature sections, students practice reading skills and identify some common literary devices.

As a writing text, *A Sense of Wonder* provides students with ideas for creative writing as well as opportunities for critical thinking and values clarification. Moreover, it emphasizes sharing and peer feedback, giving students a real audience for their work.

APPROACH

A Sense of Wonder takes the approach that giving students a genuine opportunity to experience literature and encouraging their direct, active participation in discovering literature are the best ways to engage students in the pieces. It advocates the importance of personal experience and pleasure in the teaching of literature and embraces the notion that literary pieces should also serve as models and catalysts for generating students' own creative writing.

ORGANIZATION AND TEACHING SUGGESTIONS

A Sense of Wonder is divided into six thematic units. The themes are broad and universal, addressing topics with which teachers and students everywhere can readily identify. Each unit includes four selections—consisting of one or more poems, a short story, and/or an essay or short play—that provide multiple reflections on a given theme. The selections offer a diversity of experience and opinion, allowing for comparison and contrast of different writing styles, literary elements, and ethnic and gender issues.

While the specific activities for presenting each poem, story, essay, or play vary, there is a predictable lesson format for introducing, reading, discussing, and reacting to each piece. A description of this lesson format follows, with suggestions for teaching different parts of the lesson.

Setting the Context

The purpose of this prereading section is to activate students' background knowledge regarding the theme and key ideas or issues raised in the particular literary piece. Having students share their personal experiences before they read serves several functions: it pools group knowledge, generates useful language for discussing the piece, and prepares students to make personal connections with the reading.

Discussion sections include a photo or illustration and questions. Since the purpose is to elicit students' ideas and help them share knowledge, it is suggested that you discuss these questions as a class. However, if you have a large class, some students may feel more comfortable sharing their ideas in smaller groups. In this case, you can ask each group to present its ideas to the whole class. If students seem reluctant to talk, you can "break the ice" by relating a personal experience or observation regarding one or more of the discussion questions.

Vocabulary support in the lessons with poems consists of a gloss below each poem. Providing definitions for some potentially difficult or unfamiliar words and expressions (such as idioms and slang) helps students understand and appreciate the larger meaning of the poem.

In the lessons with stories, essays, or plays—which typically include a heavier vocabulary load—a vocabulary exercise is provided in addition to the glosses. These exercises encourage students to figure out the meaning of unfamiliar words and expressions from context.

Reading the Poem, Story, Essay, or Play

The purpose of this section is to pose one or more questions for students to consider as they read the piece, giving them some aspect, feature, or idea on which to focus their attention. Students are referred back to these questions after they read and discuss the pieces to confirm their understanding.

Thinking About the Poem, Story, Essay, or Play

This section contains post-reading questions, as well as activities that focus on specific reading skills and literary elements. The activities in this section offer students guided avenues for interpretation, while giving them room to make their own personal connections to the literary pieces.

Comprehension questions check students' understanding of the main ideas and the more "objective" or literal aspects of the piece they have read. Some questions require students to identify details in the piece and to make inferences.

Focus on Reading highlights important reading skills such as getting meaning from context, making inferences, distinguishing between fact and opinion, and identifying pronoun referents. Some Focus on Reading presentations treat linguistic features as they relate to literature, such as the uses of reduced forms and register. As a class or in small groups, students read a short presentation on a specific reading skill or linguistic feature, then do an activity to practice it.

Focus on Literature helps students identify key literary elements such as metaphors, similes, personification, and alliteration. After reading a short presentation describing a particular element, students do an activity to demonstrate their understanding.

Expansion questions are interpretive and require critical thinking. They are designed to probe the more subjective aspects of the pieces. These questions lend themselves to various interpretations, and allow students to connect their personal experiences to the literature. Sometimes questions in this section deal with issues of values clarification, requiring students to reflect on their personal values as these relate to the unit themes. Because of the personal and open-ended nature of these expansion questions, it is suggested that students discuss them in small groups, where they may feel more comfortable sharing their ideas, values, and feelings.

It may sometimes happen that a student feels uncomfortable discussing—or has no opinion about—a particular question, such as one relating to personal values or perhaps some aspect of his or her culture. Accordingly, it is important to let students know that they always have the chance to opt out of discussing any question, for example by saying, "I pass," or "I have no opinion." Other students need to be encouraged to respect these responses.

Responding to the Poem, Story, Essay, or Play

These writing response activities provide a springboard and vehicle for students to connect personally and creatively with aspects and elements of the literary piece they have read. As with the previous post-reading discussion activities, the goal of these writing activities is to offer students points of departure—to suggest ways of responding to the poem, story, essay, or play—while encouraging them to use their imagination and explore their own feelings, impressions, and interpretations in crafting their personal responses.

Note that while students are given a choice of three writing response activities for each piece, you should feel free to give them the option of writing a response of their own choosing related to the piece. Since the purpose of this anthology is to encourage students to connect their experiences to literature, they should not feel restrained or discouraged from connecting creatively in their own ways with the different pieces. Of course, you may want to check a student's idea before he or she writes to make sure the response is appropriate to the piece and/or lesson theme.

Peer Response activities are pair or small group activities. Students read each other's writings, comment on them, and, as appropriate, offer suggestions for improving them. The emphasis here is on giving and receiving positive and constructive feedback—for example, pointing out what they like best about a classmate's writing, indicating if some part of the writing is unclear, or asking for more information. Moreover, by sharing their work, students are writing for a real audience—for their peers, not just for a single teacher. Finally, students stand to gain additional insights into a literary piece through their classmates' personal responses.

About the Author biographies give students information about the authors of the pieces they have read. Students who enjoy particular pieces may be moved to read other work by the authors, or to search the Internet or library for more information about particular authors.

On Further Reflection

These consolidation and extension activities appear at the end of every unit. They provide additional opportunities for students to react and relate their experiences to the different literary pieces in the unit—for example, to compare the way the characters in different pieces reacted to a similar situation, or to explore further some values that may relate to a particular theme. There are also suggestions for relating aspects of the unit theme to the community at large.

SOME NOTES ON POETRY

These notes are provided as a guide for teachers, who may find poetry the most difficult genre to introduce to students. Why is poetry considered a difficult genre? Poetry often requires very careful reading because poets use language in unusual ways to create special effects. The French poet Paul Valéry once wrote that fiction and nonfiction were like walking, but poetry was like dancing. In this sense, poets invite us to dance when we read their poems—they want us to sit up and take notice, to see and hear and feel things in new and different ways.

Poets create different effects with the form, sound, and language of their poems. Sometimes these special poetic effects may be disconcerting to readers, teachers and students alike. But they need not be. Here are notes on some key features of poetry. Keep these ideas in mind as you read the poems in this book, and use them to help your students if they have questions about aspects of the poems or about poetry in general.

- **Form** Perhaps the most unique thing about poetry, compared to other kinds of literature, is its form—the way it looks on a page. Poems are usually composed of a series of individual lines. These lines may or may not be complete sentences. In some poems, lines are grouped into separate sections, or *stanzas*. Stanzas may have the same number of lines, or the number of lines may vary.
- **Sound** Poems are meant to be read aloud, so the sound of the words is very important. Read the poems out loud to the class and then point out how poets use various techniques to create special sound effects. These techniques may include *rhyme* (the use of words with identical or similar sounds, especially at the ends of lines), *alliteration* (the repetition of consonant sounds at the beginnings of words); *rhythm* (the pattern of sound created by the arrangement of stressed and unstressed syllables in a line); and *onomatopoeia* (the use of words—like *buzz*, *bang*—whose sound indicates their meaning).

Students sometimes believe that poems must or should rhyme—that a poem isn't really a poem unless it has rhyming words, especially at the ends of lines. While many poets, both traditional and modern, use rhyme, not all poets do—particularly modern poets. In fact, as you'll see, none of the poets in this book (nor most other contemporary poets) use rhyme as a characteristic feature because their poems are written in *free verse*.

In free verse (see any of the poems in this anthology), lines and rhythm and rhyme patterns are irregular. That is, lines are long or short and words may rhyme or not, as the poet chooses. However, free verse does not mean there are *no* rules; rather, poets who write free verse make their own rules. They ask themselves questions like, "Do these lines look and feel and sound right?" The way a particular poet answers such questions determines the form of his or her free verse poem.

- **Language** Poets choose their words very carefully to create a particular mood or feeling; often, they do this to help the reader see, hear, taste, smell, or feel what is being described. This kind of sensory language and description is called *imagery*. Poets also use words to communicate ideas beyond the usual, or literal, meaning of the words. This use of words to create a special kind of meaning is called *figurative language*. Some examples of figurative language include *metaphor* (a comparison between two things), *simile* (a comparison between two things, using the words "like" or "as"), and *personification* (giving human qualities to an animal, object, or idea). See the "Focus on Literature" sections for a discussion of these literary elements. (For a complete list of literary elements presented in this book, see the Scope and Sequence on pages iv–v.)

Some Strategies for Reading Poetry

Ask students to consider these questions as they read poetry:

- **How does the poem make you feel?** Ask students to think about the way *they* feel as they read a poem. Poets create a definite feeling, or mood, in a poem through their choice of words and images. In this anthology, for example, have students compare the images Victor M. Valle uses in his poem "Food" with those Richard Hugo uses in "Blue Stone." Ask: What effect do these different images have on you? Do any images make you visualize or recall memories from your own experience? How do these images contribute to your overall feeling about the poems?
- **Who is speaking?** Have students figure out who is speaking in the poem. Poets often create vivid characters with distinct personalities. Ask: What is the character's personality, attitude, and point of view in the poem? Do you think this character is speaking for the poet? If there is more than one character, what is their relationship? For example, who is speaking in John Agard's "Wind and River Romance"?
- **What is the main idea?** Have students identify the main idea of the poem. Explain that the title may state the main idea directly, but it usually suggests an image that relates to the main idea in some way. Compare for example, the title

of Diane Kahanu's poem, "When I Was Young on an Island" with that of Gary Soto's poem, "Oranges." Ask: Which title do you think reflects the poem's main idea more directly? What lines from "Oranges" reveal the main idea?

OTHER TEACHING SUGGESTIONS

Vocabulary items may be unfamiliar. One of the underlying principles of this book is that students should be encouraged to figure out unfamiliar words and expressions from the context, and in some cases, to accept imprecise definitions. The vocabulary exercises in the lessons support this idea, and they are written to help students apply this reading strategy. To help them become more fluent and independent readers, students should be encouraged to read through the literary pieces without stopping to look up words in a dictionary. If, after reading a piece, they have questions about some words, they can use their dictionaries to look up definitions.

Student participation and group work help build students' confidence. The more comfortable students are with their peers, their teacher, and the overall classroom atmosphere, the more confident they will become in sharing their ideas and opinions as a class and in groups. Whenever possible, encourage student participation.

Another underlying principle of this book is that, in studying literature, readers' experiences and points of view are as important as those of the writers—that reading literature is a cooperative and interactive activity, wherein everyone's experience and ideas are valid in contributing to understanding the larger meaning of a piece.

Using the poems as models is a way to stimulate students' imaginations and elicit their personal connections. The poems in this anthology are intended in part to serve as models for students who wish to write their own poems. Not all students may choose to write poems, or to write poems in response to every poem. There are other writing response options included with every poem for students who choose not to write poems.

For students who do choose to write poetry, these poems will serve as springboards. The idea is not that students should try to copy or imitate the poems so much as to expand upon or experiment with whatever features and aspects of a particular poem they like. Students, whether or not they ever thought they could write poetry, may be surprised at how they can and do respond creatively to these poems. That creative response is part of the "sense of wonder" that literature has the power to evoke in all of us.

When teaching longer selections, you may want to consider having students read them in parts. For example, in Unit 1, the short story "The All-American Slurp" might be broken into two or more parts. To divide the story into two roughly equal parts, ask students to read paragraphs 1-33, then paragraphs 34-75. Alternatively, to divide the story into four parts, ask students to read paragraphs 1-19, then 20-33, then 34-58, and finally 59-75. The same may be done for other long pieces.

Share your own stories, because *A Sense of Wonder* includes pieces from many people, places, and cultures, but it is not all-inclusive. If you have a favorite poem, story, essay, or play from your own or another culture, why not share it with your class? Invite students to do the same.

ANSWER KEY

The Answer Key provides answers to the Comprehension questions, Vocabulary exercises, and for most of the Focus on Reading and Focus on Literature sections. Some of the exercises contain subjective and interpretive questions and therefore no answers for them appear in the Answer Key. Note that for some questions, possible answers are given. These are suggested interpretations, and other answers may be possible.

SUGGESTIONS FOR FURTHER READING

The following resources were most helpful and inspiring in putting together this anthology. In particular, poet and teacher Kenneth Koch's books are an essential and invaluable resource for anyone looking to find creative ways of making poetry accessible and enjoyable to *all* kinds of students, from children to older adults. For an account of how some of Koch's poetry ideas can be applied to teaching international students, including samples of students' poems, see the *TESOL Quarterly* article cited below.

Baldick, Chris. 1990. *The Concise Oxford Dictionary of Literary Terms.* New York: Oxford University Press.

Koch, Kenneth. 1970. *Wishes, Lies, and Dreams.* New York: Harper and Row.

Koch, Kenneth. 1970. *Rose, Where Did You Get that Red?* New York: Random House.

Koch, Kenneth. 1977. *I Never Told Anybody.* New York: Random House.

Koch, Kenneth and Farrell, Kate. 1982. *Sleeping on the Wing.* New York: Random House.

Padgett, Ron, editor. 1987. *The Handbook of Poetic Forms.* New York: Teachers & Writers Collaborative.

Preston, William. 1982. *Poetry Ideas in Teaching Literature and Writing to Foreign Students. TESOL Quarterly 18,* 4:489–502.

Widdowson, H.G. 1975. *Stylistics and the Teaching of Literature.* London: Longmans.

To the Student

ABOUT THIS BOOK

The title. *A Sense of Wonder* suggests that an important purpose of literature is to make us feel a sense of wonder about life. The writers in this anthology remind us that life is a special gift: one full of possibilities and full of unique and wonderful people, places, and things.

The themes. This book explores common themes that people everywhere can understand and respond to. There are six themes: Food, Love, Clothes, Growing Up, Work, and Life and Death.

The literature. The literature comes from many cultures and parts of the world, from authors male and female, young and old.

WHY READ LITERATURE?

Literature is a way to pass on good stories. All of us know good stories, but most of us don't write them down. If we don't write our stories down or tell them to others, when we die, our stories die with us. Without some written record, how will we remember the stories of our own and others' lives? How will future generations know them?

Literature connects us to something larger than ourselves. Reading literature connects us to other points of view—lets us see life through others' eyes—so that we may know and appreciate more of it. Literature lets us "walk inside other people's shoes" and discover how that feels. Literature introduces us to people so completely different from us that we discover how much we have in common.

A sense of wonder. I hope that some of the literature in this book moves and inspires you to write your own poems, stories, essays, or plays. You might even get ideas for your own book. If you do, write them down. Then you can pass on some stories— the stories you love, the stories that have inspired you, the stories that have taught you something. Enjoy!

ACKNOWLEDGMENTS

Putting together this book was a collaborative effort, requiring the contributions of many talented and creative people. I want to thank all the people who worked on this project at Pearson Education, without whose help and hard work this anthology would not exist. In particular, I thank Joanne Dresner, Allen Ascher, Louisa Hellegers, Penny Laporte, and Laura Le Dréan for believing in the original proposal. I thank Laura, especially, for supporting the project consistently and enthusiastically through to final publication, and for her crucial role in critiquing and defining the final manuscript. I also thank my two excellent editors, Lise Minovitz and Paula Van Ells, for focusing and shaping the manuscript, for their creative ideas for improving it, for clarifying ideas and eliminating redundancy. Many thanks to Mykan White for her diligent work in tracking down and getting permissions for the literary pieces in this anthology.

A number of people encouraged me before I put together a proposal for this book, and others did so as I was developing the initial manuscript. My thanks to Tom Heacox, a graduate assistant at Johns Hopkins, whose creative teaching first opened up to me the wonders of poetry and other literature, and who encouraged me to write about it. Thanks also to Ted Plaister, at the University of Hawaii at Manoa, an enthusiastic advocate of literature, who suggested to our ESL reading class that someone write a poetry anthology for ESL students. (I never forgot, though it took 20 years to do it!) Mary Freeman and Barbara Spiridon, each in their special way, encouraged me to write, and, more important, were role models for the humanistic, life-affirming vision that is at the heart of this book. Mary died in 1992, but her spirit glows brightly in these pages. I owe much gratitude to Lai Moy for her encouragement and personal contributions to an early version of this manuscript. Thanks also to my colleagues Andy Martin, Debbie Goldblatt, Jim Mentel, Ellen Northcutt, and Phyllis Dobbins for their comments on my original proposal and for encouraging me to publish it. I owe special thanks to Pamela Hartmann, Tom LaPointe, and Nela Navarro-LaPointe for using parts of this material with their students, and for their feedback and constructive ideas.

And, of course, my deepest appreciation goes to my parents, Bill and Charlotte, my wife, Mintari, and my children, Jason and Jessica, for their support, in so many ways, over the years.

About the Author

Bill Preston served as a VISTA volunteer in Yonkers, New York, from 1970–1972, where he worked as a community organizer. From 1977–1980, he was a Peace Corps volunteer in Thailand, where he taught English and supervised teachers. He has also taught English in Indonesia, Spain, and the United States. Since 1986, he has worked as an ELT editor. He currently works at Pearson Education in White Plains, New York. He holds a BA in English from Johns Hopkins University and an MA in English as a Second Language from the University of Hawaii at Manoa.

Credits

Photo credits

p. 1, © Chris Windsor/Getty Images Inc.; **p. 2,** © Catherine Karnow/CORBIS; **p. 14,** © Michael Newman/PhotoEdit; **p. 19,** © Tom Nebbia/CORBIS; **p. 34,** © Royalty Free/CORBIS; **p. 35,** © Michael Newman/PhotoEdit; **p. 42,** Courtesy of Lise Minovitz; **p. 54,** © Paul Edmondson/CORBIS; **p. 66,** © Roman Soumar/CORBIS; **p. 74,** © Nadine Markova/Corbis Stock Market; **p. 83,** © 1952, 1980 Ruth Orkin; **p. 100,** © Ken Fisher/Getty Images/Stone; **p. 101,** © Richard Hamilton Smith/CORBIS; **p. 107,** © Michelle Bridwell/PhotoEdit; **p. 118,** © Myrleen Ferguson Cate/PhotoEdit; **p. 128,** © Charles Thatcher/Getty Images Inc.; **p. 136,** © Image 100/Royalty Free/CORBIS; **p. 137,** © Jonathan Nourok/PhotoEdit; **p. 143,** © Tim Clary/AP/Wide World Photos; **p. 152,** © Roy Clark/U.S. Department of Agriculture; **p. 160,** © Andy Sacks/Getty Images Inc.; **p. 170,** © Bruce Heinemann/Getty Images, Inc./PhotoDisc, Inc.; **p. 171,** © Jeffrey L. Rotman/CORBIS; **p. 190,** © Christopher Brown/Stock Boston; **p. 197,** © Chase Swift/CORBIS

Food

*A*ccording to a popular saying, "You are what you eat." What do you eat? What are your favorite foods? Are these foods good for you? Which meal—breakfast, lunch, or dinner—do you like best?

In this unit, you will read about foods and drinks that were special to four writers for different reasons. First, poet and short story writer Sandra Cisneros remembers a special lunch she used to eat as a child. Next, essayist and travel writer Donald W. George describes the simple pleasure of drinking iced coffee in Japan. Poet Victor M. Valle reflects on several Mexican foods that are also popular in many parts of the United States. Finally, writer Lensey Namioka recalls how her family discovered differences in eating customs when they first moved to the United States from China.

As some Americans say when inviting someone to sit down and eat, "It's on the table. Help yourself."

Good Hot Dogs

SETTING THE CONTEXT

Discussion

Discuss the following questions as a class.

1. Have you ever eaten a hot dog? If so, did you put anything on it?
2. Is there any food similar to a hot dog in your country? If so, describe it.
3. Hot dogs are a popular fast food in the United States, along with hamburgers and pizza. What kinds of fast foods are popular in your country?
4. Do you like fast food? Why or why not?

READING THE POEM

As you read the poem, think about the title. What details does the poet use to show that the hot dogs were good?

Good Hot Dogs

by Sandra Cisneros
for Kiki

Fifty cents apiece[1]
To eat our lunch
We'd run
Straight from school
5 Instead of home
Two blocks
Then the store
That smelled like steam
You ordered
10 Because you had the money
Two hot dogs and two pops[2] for here[3]
Everything on the hot dogs
Except pickle lily[4]
Dash[5] those hot dogs
15 Into buns[6] and splash on
All that good stuff[7]
Yellow mustard and onions
And french fries piled on top all
Rolled up in a piece of wax
20 Paper for us to hold hot
In our hands
Quarters[8] on the counter[9]
Sit down
Good hot dogs
25 We'd eat
Fast till there was nothing left
But salt and poppy seeds even
The little burnt tips
Of french fries
30 We'd eat
You humming
And me swinging my legs

[1]**apiece** each
[2]**pop** soda pop, soft drink
[3]**for here** to eat here in the restaurant (vs. **to go**—
to take away from the restaurant)
[4]**pickle lily** a kind of sour chopped vegetable
[5]**dash** to put quickly, throw

[6]**bun** long, soft bread roll used for hot dogs
[7]**good stuff** things you enjoy
[8]**quarter** a 25-cent coin used in the United States
and Canada
[9]**counter** a long table in a restaurant where food is
served

THINKING ABOUT THE POEM

Comprehension

Discuss the following questions as a class.

1. What did the poet and her friend get for fifty cents each? Describe their lunch.
2. What "good stuff" did the poet like on her hot dog?
3. How old do you think the poet and her friend were? Why?
4. What details show that the poet and her friend enjoyed their lunch? Underline them.

Focus on Reading: Visualizing

> Writers use language in special ways to create powerful images—or pictures—in the reader's mind. You can understand the writer's feelings about a subject better when you visualize the images or try to see the pictures in your mind. For example, reread lines 3–8 in "Good Hot Dogs."
>
> > *We'd run*
> > *Straight from school*
> > *Instead of home*
> > *Two blocks*
> > *Then the store*
> > *That smelled like steam*
>
> These words create a powerful image of the poet and her friend hurrying to get hot dogs.

Underline any words or phrases in the poem that create strong pictures in your mind. Then read the poem again. Visualize the images. What kind of pictures do you see? Do the pictures help you understand the poet's feelings about hot dogs? Compare and discuss your ideas as a class.

Focus on Literature: Poetic License

> Poets use language in special and unusual ways to express their ideas and feelings. When writing poems, they often ignore the rules of conventional writing, called prose. For example, poets sometimes break grammar rules: They do not write in complete sentences or use punctuation marks. When poets break traditional writing rules, we say they are using *poetic license*.

Discuss the following questions in small groups.

1. Find examples of poetic license in "Good Hot Dogs." What rules of conventional writing does the poet break?
2. Look at how the poet breaks and arranges the lines. Do you think this affects the speed at which you read the poem? If so, how?
3. Read the poem aloud. What images, sounds, or rhythms do you think the poet is trying to emphasize or create?

Focus on Literature: Alliteration

Poets like to choose words for the way they sound together. Sometimes they repeat similar consonant sounds at the beginning of words. This is called *alliteration*. One example of alliteration in "Good Hot Dogs" is in line 4: the *-s* consonant sound is repeated in the words *Straight* and *school*. Alliteration creates rhythm through the repetition of similar sounds.

Read the poem aloud. Pay special attention to the sounds of words. What other examples of alliteration can you find?

Expansion

Discuss the following questions.

1. What is your favorite food? Describe it.
2. Why do you like it?
3. Where do you get this food? Do you buy it or make it?
4. Do you usually eat or drink anything with this food? If so, what?

RESPONDING TO THE POEM

Write about one of the following topics.

1. **A Favorite Food.** Using the poem "Good Hot Dogs" as a model, write a poem about a favorite food. Include as many details as possible. Include images that allow your reader to visualize your favorite food. Don't worry about grammar and punctuation—use poetic license! Use the following questions and your own ideas. Then give your poem a title.

- Where did you buy or eat the food?
- Did anyone go with you?
- How much did the food cost?
- Did you eat or drink anything with the food?
- Did you do anything to show that you were enjoying the food? If so, what?

2. **A Favorite Place to Eat.** Write a poem or paragraph about a favorite place to eat or get food (for example, a fast-food restaurant, a food vendor on the street, or someone's kitchen). Include as many details as possible. Include images that allow your reader to visualize the place. Use the following questions to help you.

   - Where is the place?
   - When do (or did) you go there?
   - What does the place look like?
   - How does the place smell?

3. **A Memorable Meal.** In "Good Hot Dogs," Sandra Cisneros describes a meal she remembers from her childhood. Write a poem or paragraph about a special meal you remember. Include as many details as possible. Use strong images so your readers can visualize the meal and understand why it was special.

Peer Response

Work with a partner. Exchange papers and read each other's writing. Discuss the following questions.

- What details does the writer include?
- What words or phrases create strong images?
- Does the writer use alliteration? If so, where?
- How do you think the writer feels about the topic? Why?

After you discuss your ideas, you may want to revise your writing.

About the Author

Sandra Cisneros is an American novelist, poet, and short story writer of Mexican heritage. She is especially well known for her novel, *The House on Mango Street*. She has also written a book of short stories, *Woman Hollering Creek and Other Stories*, and two books of poetry, *My Wicked, Wicked Ways* and *Loose Woman*. She lives in Texas.

The Way of Iced Coffee

SETTING THE CONTEXT

Discussion

Discuss the following questions as a class.

1. Do you like coffee? If so, how do you like to prepare it?
2. If you don't drink coffee, what drink do you like? Do you usually buy or make it? Where do you usually drink it?
3. Many people enjoy "people watching"—sitting and watching other people, especially in cafés or other places where many people walk by. Do you enjoy people watching? If so, where do you go to watch them?
4. A *ritual* is a practice that many people share. In the United States and Canada, popular food rituals include having a barbecue and going to a café for dessert. Are there any popular food rituals in your country? If so, describe them.

Vocabulary

The boldfaced words in the following sentences are from the essay on pages 9–10. Use the context to guess the meanings of the boldfaced words. Use a dictionary if necessary. Then match the boldfaced words with the correct definitions that follow. Compare your answers in small groups.

_____ 1. As I was listening to my teacher, **it struck me** that her voice sounded a lot like my aunt's.

_____ 2. The actors are **enacting** a scene from *Romeo and Juliet*.

_____ 3. At the end of the mystery, the detective **revealed** who had committed the crime.

_____ 4. Learning a second language allows you to feel more **intimately** a part of another culture.

_____ 5. Most people feel **serene** when walking in nature.

_____ 6. Sugar **dissolves** easily in hot tea or coffee.

_____ 7. The country is so divided that no leader can **unify** it.

_____ 8. We were **lingering** in the park because we didn't want to go home.

_____ 9. I **savored** the hot, delicious coffee.

_____ 10. Living in another country can **enrich** your understanding of your own country.

a. bring together as one
b. made something secret known
c. very closely
d. I suddenly realized
e. mixes with and becomes part of a liquid
f. staying longer than usual
g. enjoyed the taste or smell
h. improve
i. calm and peaceful
j. performing

READING THE ESSAY

In the title "The Way of Iced Coffee," *way* means practice or ritual. As you read the essay, think about what the author means by "The Way of Iced Coffee."

The Way of Iced Coffee
by Donald W. George

1   Three months ago I was sitting in a Tokyo coffee shop, lingering over a glass of iced coffee and watching the world go by. I was smiling at everything and nothing, sipping my iced coffee, watching the people passing outside and the people sipping inside, and suddenly it struck me that one reason for my sense of well-being was the little ritual I was enacting—a ritual I had been enacting ever since my first sip of iced coffee ten years before.

2   As I reflected on this, I realized that I had seen variations of this ritual enacted—unconsciously—in countless Japanese coffee shops by countless people, and that in fact the preparation and drinking of iced coffee had become one of those delightful little rites[1] that unify and enrich Japanese life.

3   To my knowledge, however, no one had recognized it as such, so I decided to order another iced coffee and to set down my own modest version of *aisu kohido*, "the way of iced coffee."

4   To enjoy this simple rite, you need first to install yourself in a comfortable coffee shop, then order by saying, "*Aisu kohi, kudasai.*"[2] What follows probably won't reveal any profound truths, but it may make you feel more intimately a part of the mesh[3] of modern Japan—and it will certainly provide a welcome chance to relax and reflect in the middle of a hard sightseeing day.

5   When your iced coffee is placed before you, study it for a while: the dark, rich liquid glistens[4] with ice cubes whose curves and cracks hold and reflect and refract[5] the liquid.

6   Notice the thin silver streaks and peaks in the ice cubes, and the beads of water on the outside of the glass—a cooling sight on a hot day. Then take up the tiny silver pitcher of sugar syrup[6] that has been set just beside the glass and pour it into the part of the glass that is nearest to you. The syrupy stream courses through the coffee like a tiny waterfall, then quickly disperses[7] and dissolves, like the dream of a rain shower on a summer afternoon.

7   After that, pick up the tiny white pitcher of cream that was placed just beyond the silver pitcher and pour it into the middle of the glass. Watch it

---

[1]**rite** a ceremony, a ritual
[2]**Aisu kohi, kudasai.** *(Japanese)* Iced coffee, please.
[3]**mesh** a combination of people, ideas, or things
[4]**glisten** to shine, appear wet or oily

[5]**refract** to make light change direction when it passes through a glass or water
[6]**syrup** a thick, sweet liquid
[7]**disperse** to mix with and become part of a liquid

disperse into countless cream-colored swirls and whirls and streams, which hang suspended in the middle of the coffee like a frozen breeze. Notice how the cream is pure white in some parts and a thin brownish hue in others. Notice also that a little trace stays on the surface, spiraling down into the middle of the glass.

8   Then unwrap the straw that has been set beyond the glass and place it in the middle of the glass. This sends out ripples that reconfigure the cream's liquid breeze, creating new waves and textures and layers of iced coffee.

9   Finally, after appreciating this effect to your satisfaction, stir the coffee vigorously with your straw—the ice cubes clinking like wind chimes in a seaside breeze—until the coffee is a uniform sand-colored hue.

10   Then sip the coffee through the straw, tasting its coolness and complex mix of bitter coffee and sweet sugar and cream.

11   Now sit back, sip, and watch the world go by—smiling and serene that pleasure can sometimes be savored in such simple things.

THINKING ABOUT THE ESSAY

Comprehension

Discuss the following questions as a class.

1. What was the author doing at the beginning of the essay?
2. How was he feeling? Why?
3. What did the author suddenly realize?
4. Why do you think the author says preparing and drinking iced coffee is a ritual?
5. What is the author's purpose in writing "The Way of Iced Coffee"?

Focus on Reading: Sequence Words

Writers use words such as *first, then, after that, finally,* and *now* to indicate the order of events in a series or the steps in a process. These are called *sequence words.*

The following sentences are from the essay. Underline the sequence words. Then put the sentences in the correct order. Reread the essay if necessary. Write the numbers on the lines.

_____ Then unwrap the straw and place it in the middle of the glass.

_*1*_ To enjoy this simple rite, you need first to install yourself in a comfortable coffee shop, then order by saying, "*Aisu kohi, kudasai.*"

_____ Now sit back, sip, and watch the world go by.

_____ After that, pick up the tiny white pitcher of cream and pour it into the middle of the glass.

_____ Finally, stir the coffee vigorously with your straw until the coffee is a uniform sand-colored hue.

_____ Then take up the tiny silver pitcher of sugar syrup and pour it into the part of the glass that is nearest to you.

Focus on Literature: Similes

> Sometimes writers compare things in unusual ways to create strong images. When these comparisons use the words *like* or *as*, they are called *similes*. Look at the following sentences.
>
>   *The steak is tough.*
>
>   *The **steak** is as tough as **leather**.*
>
> The second statement has a simile. Notice how it creates a strong image.

A. Work with a partner. Reread paragraphs 6–9. Find the similes and underline them. Then complete the following sentences.

1. In paragraph 6, ___*the syrupy stream*___ is compared to ___*a tiny waterfall*___ .

2. In paragraph 6, _____ is compared to _____ .

3. In paragraph 7, _____ is compared to _____ .

4. In paragraph 9, _____ is compared to _____ .

B. Which simile do you like best? Why?

Expansion

Discuss the following questions.

1. Yogi Berra was a famous catcher for the New York Yankees baseball team. People also remember him for his humorous sayings about life. One of his famous sayings is, "You can observe a lot by watching." Do you agree or disagree? Explain.
2. How does this saying relate to the essay?
3. How does this saying relate to your experience? Did you ever learn something by observing or watching? If so, give an example.

RESPONDING TO THE ESSAY

Write about one of the following topics.

1. **A Favorite Food Ritual.** Write a paragraph or essay about a favorite food ritual. Be sure to explain clearly the steps in the ritual. Use the following questions to help you.

    - What special food or drink do you prepare?
    - Do you eat or drink it in a special place?
    - Why is this food or drink special?
    - Do other people perform this food ritual too?

2. **Beginner's Mind.** *Beginner's mind* refers to looking at a familiar practice as if seeing it for the first time. For example, in "The Way of Iced Coffee," the author describes the familiar practice of preparing and drinking iced coffee as if looking at it for the first time. Use beginner's mind to describe a familiar practice. Look at the practice and describe it as if you are seeing it for the first time. If describing a sequence of events, be sure to use sequence words.

3. **Simple Pleasures.** In "The Way of Iced Coffee," the author suddenly realizes the simple pleasure of preparing and drinking iced coffee, something he has done for years. Describe an activity that *you* consider to be a simple pleasure. Why do you enjoy it? How does it make you feel? Use sequence words and similes if possible.

Peer Response

Work with a partner. Exchange papers and read each other's writing. Discuss the following questions.

- Does the writer use any similes?
- Does the writer use sequence words?
- Do you have any questions for the writer?
- What do you like best about the writing?

After you discuss your ideas, you may want to revise your writing.

About the Author

Donald W. George was the Travel Editor at the *San Francisco Examiner* for eight years. His award-winning essays and articles have appeared in publications around the world. He is the editor of *Salon.com's Wanderlust: Real-Life Tales of Adventure and Romance.* "The Way of Iced Coffee" originally appeared in the *San Francisco Examiner.* It can also be found in a collection of travel writing called *Food: True Stories of Life on the Road.*

Food

SETTING THE CONTEXT

Discussion

Discuss the following questions as a class.

1. Three foods that are traditional in Mexico and the southwestern United States are *tortillas*, *frijoles*, and *chiles*. Tortillas are a kind of thin bread made from cornmeal or flour. Frijoles are brown or black beans that are often mashed and fried. Chiles are peppers that are usually hot and spicy. Have you ever eaten these foods? If so, where?

2. What foods are traditional in your country? Describe them.

3. In the United States, many people eat bread with their meals. Do people usually eat bread with meals in your country? If not, what do they eat instead?

4. Most Mexican food is spicy. How would you describe the food in your country? If it is spicy, what do people use to make the food spicy?

READING THE POEM

As you read the poem, notice how four foods are compared with parts of nature. How are they similar?

Food

by Victor M. Valle

One eats
the moon in a tortilla
Eat frijoles
and you eat the earth
5   Eat chile
and you eat sun and fire
Drink water
and you drink sky

Comprehension

Notice the verb forms and subject pronouns in "Food." These forms express particular ideas and feelings about the four foods. If Victor M. Valle had used the simple past and himself as the subject in the poem, the poem would look like this:

I ate
the moon in a tortilla
I ate frijoles
and I ate the earth
I ate chile
and I ate sun and fire
I drank water
and I drank sky

Discuss the following questions as a class.

1. Why do you think the poet did not use himself as the subject of this poem?
2. Who is the poet referring to with the pronouns *One* and *you*?
3. Why do you think he chose the simple present instead of the simple past? How does the meaning of the poem change if the verbs are in the past?

Focus on Literature: Metaphors

> Remember that a simile compares one thing to another thing by suggesting that it is *like* or *as* the other thing. Writers also use *metaphors* to make comparisons. However, a metaphor compares two things without using the words *like* or *as*. Look at the following two sentences.
>
> > Jack has a **heart** of **stone**.
> >
> > Jill has a **heart** of **gold**.
>
> Each sentence has a metaphor; it compares a person's heart to something else without using *like* or *as*.

A. Work with a partner. Find the metaphors the poet uses for four foods. Write each food, aspect of nature, and similarity in the chart. (**Note:** The third metaphor compares one food to two other aspects of nature.)

Food	Part of Nature	Similarity
tortilla	moon	round

B. Discuss the metaphors. Do you agree with all the comparisons? Why or why not?

Expansion

1. In "Food," Victor M. Valle writes about foods that are very important to him. What foods are very important to you? Write your answers in the chart that follows.
2. Work in groups of four. Ask your classmates what foods are very important to them. Write their answers in the chart.
3. Compare and discuss your answers. Why are these foods so important? If you moved to a place that didn't have these foods, which one would you miss most? Why?

You	Student 1	Student 2	Student 3
1.	1.	1.	1.
2.	2.	2.	2.
3.	3.	3.	3.
4.	4.	4.	4.

RESPONDING TO THE POEM

Write about one of the following topics.

1. **Favorite Foods Poem.** Write a poem about some foods that you really like. Use the poem "Food" as a model. Use the following steps to help you write your poem.

   • Make a chart comparing each food to something else. Write the food, the other thing, and the similarity. Follow the example.

Food	Other thing	Similarity
soup	volcano	very hot, steaming

   • Write metaphors to compare each food or drink to another thing. (For example: *Hot soup is a steaming volcano. A pizza is a flying saucer.*)
   • Write a poem using your food metaphors.
   • Give your poem a title.

2. **A Group Food Poem.** Write metaphors about your favorite foods. Then work in small groups. Choose the metaphors you like best. Write a group poem, using one metaphor from each student.

3. **Important Foods.** Write a paragraph or essay about a food or drink that is very important to you. Describe the food or drink and explain why it is important. If possible, use metaphors in your description.

Peer Response

Work with a partner. Exchange papers and read each other's writing.* Discuss the following questions.

- Does the writer use metaphors?
- What did you learn about a food or drink?
- Do you understand why the writer finds the food or drink important?
- Do you have any questions for the writer?
- What do you like best about the writing?

After you discuss your ideas, you might want to revise your writing.

* (**Note:** If you wrote a group food poem, share your poem with the class.)

About the Author

Victor M. Valle was born in California in 1950. In addition to writing poetry, he has worked as a newspaper reporter, translator, editor, and community activist. He wrote, "Poetry is a tool because it helps you take things apart." His recent books include *Recipe of Memory: Five Generations of Mexican Family Cuisine* and *Latino Metropolis*.

The All-American Slurp

SETTING THE CONTEXT

Discussion

Discuss the following questions as a class.

1. What do you see on the table in the picture?
2. Have you ever eaten a traditional Chinese meal? Have you ever used chopsticks? If so, describe the experience.
3. Have you ever eaten with a group of people and been unfamiliar with their eating customs? If so, describe the experience.

Vocabulary

The boldfaced words in the following sentences are from the story on pages 21–29. Use the context to guess the meanings of the boldfaced words. Use a dictionary if necessary. Then match the boldfaced words with the correct definitions that follow. Compare your answers in small groups.

_____ 1. I had **a hard time** with mathematics at first, but later it became easier.

_____ 2. Parents want their children to have good **manners**, such as saying "please."

_____ 3. In old, torn clothing, the rich king **passed for** a poor beggar.

_____ 4. When I dropped my plate in the cafeteria, I felt like I had **made a spectacle** of myself.

_____ 5. When the boss gave his niece a big promotion, some people thought he was **showing favoritism**.

_____ 6. John is very intelligent, and he likes to **show off** by talking about his grades.

_____ 7. My father **resolved** to stop smoking last month, and he hasn't smoked since.

_____ 8. We wanted to go to the beach, but it rained so we **wound up** staying home.

_____ 9. When our team won the game, we all cheered **in unison**.

_____10. Our teacher never calls on us in any special order. Instead, she calls on us **at random**.

a. unfairly giving better treatment
b. polite ways of behaving in social situations
c. difficulty
d. promised or decided to do something
e. looked like
f. did something without wanting to
g. at the same time, together
h. done something embarrassing
i. in an unplanned way
j. try to make people notice and admire

READING THE STORY

In "The All-American Slurp," the author recalls her early experiences with American table manners. As you read, think about the three dinners she describes—at the Gleasons, at the restaurant, and at her home. How are they similar? How are they different?

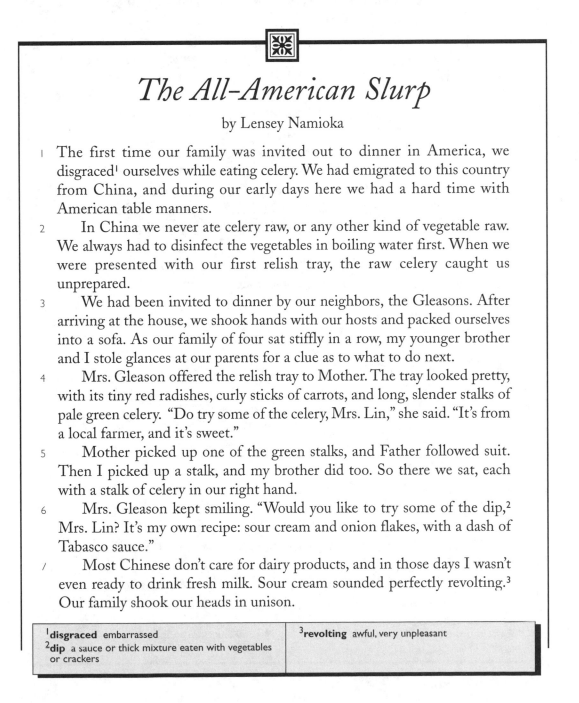

The All-American Slurp

by Lensey Namioka

1   The first time our family was invited out to dinner in America, we disgraced[1] ourselves while eating celery. We had emigrated to this country from China, and during our early days here we had a hard time with American table manners.

2   In China we never ate celery raw, or any other kind of vegetable raw. We always had to disinfect the vegetables in boiling water first. When we were presented with our first relish tray, the raw celery caught us unprepared.

3   We had been invited to dinner by our neighbors, the Gleasons. After arriving at the house, we shook hands with our hosts and packed ourselves into a sofa. As our family of four sat stiffly in a row, my younger brother and I stole glances at our parents for a clue as to what to do next.

4   Mrs. Gleason offered the relish tray to Mother. The tray looked pretty, with its tiny red radishes, curly sticks of carrots, and long, slender stalks of pale green celery. "Do try some of the celery, Mrs. Lin," she said. "It's from a local farmer, and it's sweet."

5   Mother picked up one of the green stalks, and Father followed suit. Then I picked up a stalk, and my brother did too. So there we sat, each with a stalk of celery in our right hand.

6   Mrs. Gleason kept smiling. "Would you like to try some of the dip,[2] Mrs. Lin? It's my own recipe: sour cream and onion flakes, with a dash of Tabasco sauce."

7   Most Chinese don't care for dairy products, and in those days I wasn't even ready to drink fresh milk. Sour cream sounded perfectly revolting.[3] Our family shook our heads in unison.

---

[1]**disgraced** embarrassed
[2]**dip** a sauce or thick mixture eaten with vegetables or crackers

[3]**revolting** awful, very unpleasant

8   Mrs. Gleason went off with the relish tray to the other guests, and we carefully watched to see what they did. Everyone seemed to eat the raw vegetables quite happily.

9   Mother took a bite of her celery. *Crunch.* "It's not bad," she whispered.

10   Father took a bite of his celery. *Crunch.* "Yes, it's good," he said, looking surprised.

11   I took a bite, and then my brother. *Crunch, crunch.* It was more than good; it was delicious. Raw celery has a slight sparkle, a zingy taste that you don't get in cooked celery. When Mrs. Gleason came around with the relish tray, we each took another stalk of celery, except my brother. He took two.

12   There was only one problem: long strings ran through the length of the stalk, and they got caught in my teeth. When I help my mother in the kitchen, I always pull the strings out before slicing celery.

13   I pulled the strings out of my stalk. *Z-z-zip, z-z-zip.* My brother followed suit. *Z-z-zip, z-z-zip.* To my left, my parents were taking care of their own stalks. *Z-z-zip, z-z-zip, z-z-zip.*

14   Suddenly I realized that there was dead silence except for our zipping. Looking up, I saw that the eyes of everyone were on our family. Mr. and Mrs. Gleason, their daughter Meg, who was my friend, and their neighbors the Badels—they were all staring at us as we busily pulled the strings of our celery.

15   That wasn't the end of it. Mrs. Gleason announced that dinner was served and invited us to the dining table. It was lavishly covered with platters of food, but we couldn't see any chairs around the table. So we helpfully carried over some dining chairs and sat down. All the other guests just stood there.

16   Mrs. Gleason bent down and whispered to us, "This is a buffet dinner. You help yourselves to some food and eat it in the living room."

17   Our family beat a retreat[4] back to the sofa as if chased by enemy soldiers. For the rest of the evening, too mortified[5] to go back to the dining table, I nursed a bit of potato salad on my plate.

18   Next day Meg and I got on the school bus together. I wasn't sure how she would feel about me after the spectacle our family made at the party. But she was just the same as usual, and the only reference she made to the party was, "Hope you and your folks got enough to eat last night. You

---

[4]**beat a retreat** left quickly, as if afraid or embarrassed

[5]**mortified** ashamed, embarrassed

certainly didn't take very much. Mom never tries to figure out how much food to prepare. She just puts everything on the table and hopes for the best."

19   I began to relax. The Gleasons' dinner party wasn't so different from a Chinese meal after all. My mother also puts everything on the table and hopes for the best.

20   Meg was the first friend I had made after we came to America. I eventually got acquainted with a few other kids in school, but Meg was still the only real friend I had.

21   My brother didn't have any problems making friends. He spent all his time with some boys who were teaching him baseball, and in no time he could speak English much faster than I could—not better, but faster.

22   I worried more about making mistakes, and I spoke carefully, making sure I could say everything right before opening my mouth. At least I had a better accent than my parents, who never really got rid of their Chinese accent, even years later. My parents had both studied English in school before coming to America, but what they had studied was mostly written English, not spoken.

23   Father's approach to English was a scientific one. Since Chinese verbs have no tense, he was fascinated by the way English verbs changed form according to whether they were in the present, past imperfect, perfect, pluperfect, future, or future perfect tense. He was always making diagrams of verbs and their inflections, and he looked for opportunities to show off his mastery of the pluperfect and future perfect tenses, his two favorites. "I shall have finished my project by Monday," he would say smugly.

24   Mother's approach was to memorize lists of polite phrases that could cover all possible situations. She was constantly muttering things like "I'm fine, thank you. And you?" Once she accidentally stepped on someone's foot, and hurriedly blurted,[6] "Oh, that's quite all right!" Embarrassed by her slip,[7] she resolved to do better next time. So when someone stepped on *her* foot, she cried, "You're welcome!"

25   In our different ways, we made progress in learning English. But I had another worry, and that was my appearance. My brother didn't have to worry, since Mother bought him blue jeans for school, and he dressed like all the other boys. But she insisted that girls had to wear skirts. By the time she saw that Meg and the other girls were wearing jeans, it was too late.

---

[6]blurted said suddenly without thinking   **[7]slip** a mistake

My school clothes were bought already, and we didn't have money left to buy new outfits[8] for me. We had too many other things to buy first, like furniture, pots, and pans.

26   The first time I visited Meg's house, she took me upstairs to her room, and I wound up trying on her clothes. We were pretty much the same size, since Meg was shorter and thinner than average. Maybe that's how we became friends in the first place. Wearing Meg's jeans and T-shirt, I looked at myself in the mirror. I could almost pass for an American—from the back, anyway. At least kids in school wouldn't stop and stare at me in the hallways, which was what they did when they saw me in my white blouse and navy blue skirt that went a couple of inches below the knees.

27   When Meg came to my house, I invited her to try on my Chinese dresses, the ones with the high collar and slits[9] up the sides. Meg's eyes were bright as she looked at herself in the mirror. She struck several sultry poses,[10] and we nearly fell over laughing.

28   The dinner party at the Gleasons' didn't stop my growing friendship with Meg. Things were getting better for me in other ways too. Mother finally bought me some jeans at the end of the month, when Father got his paycheck. She wasn't in any hurry about buying them at first, until I worked on her. This is what I did. Since we didn't have a car in those days, I often ran down to the neighborhood store to pick up things for her. The groceries cost less at a big supermarket, but the closest one was many blocks away. One day, when she ran out of flour, I offered to borrow a bike from our neighbor's son and buy a ten-pound bag of flour at the big supermarket. I mounted the boy's bike and waved to mother. "I'll be back in five minutes!"

29   Before I started pedaling, I heard her voice behind me. "You can't go out in public like that! People can see all the way up to your thighs!"

30   "I'm sorry," I said innocently. "I thought you were in a hurry to get the flour." For dinner we were going to have pot-stickers (fried Chinese dumplings), and we needed a lot of flour.

31   "Couldn't you borrow a girl's bicycle?" complained Mother. "That way your skirt won't be pushed up."

32   "There aren't too many of those around," I said. "Almost all the girls wear jeans while riding a bike, so they don't see any point buying a girl's bike."

---

[8]**outfit** a set of clothing worn together
[9]**slit** a long narrow cut or opening

[10]**struck poses** stood or sat in different positions

33   We didn't eat pot-stickers that evening, and Mother was thoughtful. Next day we took the bus downtown and she bought me a pair of jeans. In the same week, my brother made the baseball team of his junior high school, and Father started taking driving lessons, and Mother discovered rummage sales.[11] We soon got all the furniture we needed, plus a dart board and a 1,000-piece jigsaw puzzle (fourteen hours later, we discovered that it was a 999-piece jigsaw puzzle). There was hope that the Lins might become a normal family after all.

34   Then came our dinner at the Lakeview restaurant.

35   The Lakeview was an expensive restaurant, one of those places where a headwaiter dressed in tails conducted you to your seat, and the only light came from candles and flaming desserts. In one corner of the room a lady harpist played tinkling melodies.

36   Father wanted to celebrate, because he had just been promoted. He worked for an electronics company, and after his English started improving, his superiors decided to appoint him to a position more suited to his training. The promotion not only brought a higher salary but was also a tremendous boost to his pride.

37   Up to then we had eaten only in Chinese restaurants. Although my brother and I were becoming fond of hamburgers, my parents didn't care much for western food, other than chow mein.[12]

38   But this was a special occasion, and Father asked his coworkers to recommend a really elegant restaurant. So there we were at the Lakeview, stumbling after the headwaiter in the murky[13] dining room.

39   At our table we were handed our menus, and they were so big that to read mine I almost had to stand up again. But why bother? It was mostly in French, anyway.

40   Father, being an engineer, was always systematic. He took out a pocket French dictionary. "They told me that most of the items would be in French, so I came prepared." He even had a pocket flashlight, the size of a marking pen. While Mother held the flashlight over the menu, he looked up the items that were in French.

41   "*Pâté en croûte,*" he muttered. "Let's see . . . *pâté* is paste . . . *croûte* is crust . . . hmm . . . a paste in crust."

42   The waiter stood looking impatient. I squirmed[14] and died at least fifty times.

---

[11]**rummage sale** an event at which used clothes, toys, and other items are sold
[12]**chow mein** a Chinese-American dish usually made with meat, vegetables, and noodles

[13]**murky** dark
[14]**squirm** to twist one's body because uncomfortable or nervous

43   At long last Father gave up. "Why don't we just order four complete dinners at random?" he suggested.

44   "Isn't that risky?" asked Mother. "The French eat some rather peculiar[15] things, I've heard."

45   "A Chinese can eat anything a Frenchman can eat," Father declared.

46   The soup arrived in a plate. How do you get soup up from a plate? I glanced at the other diners, but the ones at nearby tables were not on their soup course, while the more distant ones were invisible in the darkness.

47   Fortunately my parents had studied books on western etiquette[16] before they came to America. "Tilt your plate," whispered my mother. "It's easier to spoon the soup up that way."

48   She was right. Tilting the plate did the trick. But the etiquette book didn't say anything about what you did after the soup reached your lips. As any respectable Chinese knows, the correct way to eat your soup is to slurp. This helps to cool the liquid and prevent you from burning your lips. It also shows your appreciation.

49   We showed our appreciation, *Shloop*, went my father. *Shloop*, went my mother. *Shloop, shloop*, went my brother, who was the hungriest.

50   The lady harpist stopped playing to take a rest. And in the silence, our family's consumption of soup suddenly seemed unnaturally loud. You know how it sounds on a rocky beach when the tide goes out and the water drains from all those little pools? They go *shloop, shloop, shloop*. That was the Lin family, eating soup.

51   At the next table a waiter was pouring wine. When a large *shloop* reached him, he froze. The bottle continued to pour, and red wine flooded the tabletop and into the lap of a customer. Even the customer didn't notice anything at first, being also hypnotized by the *shloop, shloop, shloop*.

52   It was too much. "I need to go to the toilet," I mumbled, jumping to my feet. A waiter, sensing my urgency, quickly directed me to the ladies' room.

53   I splashed cold water on my burning face, and as I dried myself with a paper towel, I stared into the mirror. In this perfumed ladies' room, with its pink-and-silver wallpaper and marble sinks, I looked completely out of place. What was I doing here? What was our family doing in the Lakeview restaurant? In America?

54   The door to the ladies' room opened. A woman came in and glanced curiously at me. I retreated into one of the toilet cubicles and latched the door.

---

[15]**peculiar** strange, unusual   [16]**etiquette** formal rules for polite behavior

55   Time passed—maybe half an hour, maybe an hour. Then I heard the door open again, and my mother's voice. "Are you in there? You're not sick, are you?"

56   There was real concern in her voice. A girl can't leave her family just because they slurp their soup. Besides, the toilet cubicle had a few drawbacks[17] as a permanent residence. "I'm all right," I said, undoing the latch.

57   Mother didn't tell me how the rest of the dinner went, and I didn't want to know. In the weeks following, I managed to push the whole thing into the back of my mind, where it jumped out at me only a few times a day. Even now, I turn hot all over when I think of the Lakeview restaurant.

58   But by the time we had been in this country for three months, our family was definitely making progress toward becoming Americanized. I remember my parents' first PTA[18] meeting. Father wore a neat suit and tie, and Mother put on her first pair of high heels. She stumbled only once. They met my homeroom teacher and beamed as she told them that I would make honor roll[19] soon at the rate I was going. Of course Chinese etiquette forced Father to say that I was a very stupid girl and Mother to protest that the teacher was showing favoritism toward me. But I could tell they were both very proud.

59   The day came when my parents announced that they wanted to give a dinner party. We had invited Chinese friends to eat with us before, but this dinner was going to be different. In addition to a Chinese-American family, we were going to invite the Gleasons.

60   "Gee, I can hardly wait to have dinner at your house," Meg said to me. "I just love Chinese food."

61   That was a relief. Mother was a good cook, but I wasn't sure if people who ate sour cream would also eat chicken gizzards[20] stewed in soy sauce.

62   Mother decided not to take a chance with the chicken gizzards. Since we had western guests, she set the table with large dinner plates, which we never use in Chinese meals. In fact we didn't use individual plates at all, but picked up food from the platters in the middle of the table and brought it directly to our rice bowls. Following the practice of Chinese-American restaurants, Mother also placed large serving spoons on the platters.

---

[17]**drawback** a disadvantage, a problem
[18]**PTA** Parent-Teacher Association, a group of parents and teachers that works to improve schools

[19]**honor roll** a list of students who receive the highest grades in school
[20]**gizzards** internal organs of birds

63   The dinner started well. Mrs. Gleason exclaimed at the beautifully arranged dishes of food: the colorful candied fruit in the sweet-and-sour pork dish, the noodle-thin shreds of chicken meat stir-fried with tiny peas, and the glistening pink prawns in a ginger sauce.

64   At first I was too busy enjoying my food to notice how the guests were doing. But soon I remembered my duties. Sometimes guests were too polite to help themselves and you had to serve them with more food.

65   I glanced at Meg, to see if she needed more food, and my eyes nearly popped out at the sight of her plate. It was piled with food: the sweet-and-sour meat pushed right against the chicken shreds, and the chicken sauce ran into the prawns. She had been taking food from a second dish before she finished eating her helping from the first!

66   Horrified, I turned to look at Mrs. Gleason. She was dumping rice out of her bowl and putting it on her dinner plate. Then she ladled prawns and gravy on top of the rice and mixed everything together, the way you mix sand, gravel, and cement to make concrete.

67   I couldn't bear to look any longer, and I turned to Mr. Gleason. He was chasing a pea around his plate. Several times he got it to the edge, but when he tried to pick it up with his chopsticks, it rolled back toward the center of the plate again. Finally he put down the chopsticks and picked up the pea with his fingers. He really did! A grown man!

68   All of us, our family and the Chinese guests, stopped eating to watch the activities of the Gleasons. I wanted to giggle.[21] Then I caught my mother's eyes on me. She frowned and shook her head slightly, and I understood the message: the Gleasons were not used to Chinese ways, and they were just coping[22] the best they could. For some reason I thought of celery strings.

69   When the main courses were finished, Mother brought out a platter of fruit. "I hope you weren't expecting a sweet dessert," she said. "Since the Chinese don't eat dessert, I didn't think to prepare any."

70   "Oh, I couldn't possibly eat dessert!" cried Mrs. Gleason. "I'm simply stuffed!"

71   Meg had different ideas. When the table was cleared, she announced that she and I were going for a walk. "I don't know about you, but I feel like a dessert," she told me, when we were outside. "Come on, there's a Dairy Queen[23] down the street. I could use a big chocolate milkshake!"[24]

[21]**giggle** to laugh quietly
[22]**coping** dealing with a problem successfully

[23]**Dairy Queen** an American fast-food restaurant that sells ice cream
[24]**milkshake** a drink made of milk and ice cream

72   Although I didn't really want anything more to eat, I insisted on paying for the milkshakes. After all, I was still hostess.

73   Meg got her large chocolate milkshake and I had a small one. Even so, she was finishing hers while I was only half done. Toward the end she pulled hard on her straws and went *shloop, shloop*.

74   "Do you always slurp when you eat a milkshake?" I asked, before I could stop myself.

75   Meg grinned. "Sure. All Americans slurp."

THE ALL-AMERICAN SLURP, by Lensey Namioka, copyright © 1987, from VISIONS, ed. by Donald R. Gallo. Reprinted by permission of Lensey Namioka.

THINKING ABOUT THE STORY

Comprehension

Discuss the following questions in small groups.

1. What mistakes did the Lin family make at the Gleasons' dinner party? How did they feel?
2. What mistakes did they make at the Lakeview restaurant? How did the narrator feel?
3. What mistakes did the Gleason family make at the Lins' dinner party? Do you think the Gleasons noticed their mistakes? Explain.
4. Explain the title "The All-American Slurp." How does it relate to the story?

Focus on Reading: Guessing Meaning from Context

Often you can guess the meaning of a word by looking at the words around it. This is called guessing meaning from context. For example, look at the following sentences from the story.

*In China we never ate **celery raw**, or any other kind of vegetable raw. We always had to **disinfect** the vegetables in boiling water first.*

If you don't know the meaning of *celery*, the words after it show that it's a *kind of vegetable*. If you don't know the meaning of *raw*, the words *in boiling water* give you a clue that it means not cooked. Information in both sentences can help you guess the meaning of *disinfect*. The fact that the people in China never ate vegetables raw because they always boiled them in water first gives you clues that disinfect means to clean something in order to destroy bacteria.

The following sentences are from the story. Use the context to guess the meaning of the boldfaced words. Write definitions.

1. Mother picked up one of the green stalks, and Father **followed suit**. Then I picked up a stalk, and my brother did too.

   followed suit: _did the same thing as someone else_

2. "This is a **buffet dinner**. You help yourselves to some food and eat it in the living room."

   buffet dinner: _____

3. Meg was the first friend I had made after we came to America. I eventually **got acquainted with** a few other **kids** in school, but Meg was still the only real friend I had.

   got acquainted with: _____

   kids: _____

4. The **promotion** not only brought a higher salary but was also a tremendous boost to his pride.

   promotion: _____

5. "Oh, I couldn't possibly eat dessert!" cried Mrs. Gleason. "I'm simply **stuffed**!"

   stuffed: _____

Focus on Literature: Onomatopoeia

> Writers sometimes use or create words that sound like the actions or things they describe. This is called *onomatopoeia*. Some examples of onomatopoeia are:
>
> *fizz* (the sound of gas bubbles in a drink)
>
> *hiss* (the sound a snake makes)
>
> *whoosh* (the sound of something moving very fast, such as a car)

1. Find three examples of onomatopoeia in the story. What do they describe?
2. Does your native language use onomatopoeia? If so, share some examples with your classmates. Can your classmates guess what the words describe?

Expansion

A. Check (✓) your answers to the questions. Then discuss your answers in small groups. Which answers are similar? Which answers are different?

For dinner, do you . . .	Always	Usually	Sometimes	Never
eat food on a plate?	☐	☐	☐	☐
eat food in a bowl?	☐	☐	☐	☐
use knives, forks, or spoons?	☐	☐	☐	☐
use chopsticks?	☐	☐	☐	☐
use your fingers to eat?	☐	☐	☐	☐
eat everything before taking more food?	☐	☐	☐	☐
mix food together on your plate/in your bowl?	☐	☐	☐	☐
eat each food dish separately?	☐	☐	☐	☐
eat something sweet for dessert?	☐	☐	☐	☐
slurp your drink?	☐	☐	☐	☐
slurp your soup?	☐	☐	☐	☐
burp after or while eating?	☐	☐	☐	☐

B. Discuss the following questions.

1. Have you ever eaten a meal in another culture and done something that was inappropriate in that culture? If so, what was it? How did the others react? How did you feel? What did you learn?
2. Mr. Lin ordered four dinners at random because he didn't understand the menu. Have you ever ordered a meal when you didn't understand the menu? If so, what happened?

RESPONDING TO THE STORY

Write about one of the following topics.

1. **A Food Experience.** Write about a funny or embarrassing food experience. Use onomatopoeia if appropriate. Consider the following questions.

   • What happened? Why was it funny or embarrassing?
   • How did other people react?
   • What did you learn?

2. **Eating Customs.** Eating customs vary. What is normal or polite in one culture may be considered strange or impolite in another. For example, in some cultures burping during a meal shows appreciation of the food. In other cultures burping during a meal is considered rude. Write a paragraph or essay comparing eating customs in your country with customs in another country.

3. **A Dinner Party.** Write a paragraph or essay describing a dinner party you attended. Think about the following questions.

   • What special foods were served?
   • What special dishes or utensils were used?
   • Were any special rules of etiquette used? If so, explain them.

Peer Response

Work with a partner. Exchange papers and read each other's writing. Discuss the following questions.

   • Are there any words you don't understand? If so, can you guess the meaning from context?
   • Does the writer use any onomatopoeia?
   • Did you learn anything about eating customs? If so, what did you learn?
   • Do you have any questions for the writer?
   • What do you like best about the writing?

After you discuss your ideas, you may want to revise your writing.

About the Author

Lensey Namioka was born in Beijing, China. Her family moved to the United States in the 1940s, when she was nine years old. She is the author of many books, including *Village of the Vampire Cat*, *Who's Hu?* and *The Hungriest Boy in the World*. Her story "The All-American Slurp" appears in a collection of multicultural stories called *America Street*. She lives in Seattle, Washington.

ON FURTHER REFLECTION

Making Connections

Discuss the following questions.

1. Each writer in this unit shared an experience related to food. Which experience did you enjoy most? Why?
2. If you could have lunch with one of the writers in this unit, which person would you choose? Explain.
3. If you could eat at the store from "Good Hot Dogs," drink at the coffee shop from "The Way of Iced Coffee," or dine at the French reataurant from "The All-American Slurp," which one would you choose? Why?

Connecting to the Community

Choose one of the following projects.

1. Many people do not have enough food to eat. Does your community have any organizations that help the hungry—for example, places that provide meals for homeless people? Look in the phone book under community services, call your local government offices, or check the Internet. Find out if there is an organization that needs volunteers. If so, ask what the volunteers do and how you can help. Report your findings to the class.
2. Many communities have food banks—organizations that collect food from community members and distribute it to people who don't have enough food to eat. Does your community have a food bank? To find out, look in the phone book, call your local government, or check the Internet. If there is a food bank, find out what kinds of food are needed. As a class, collect food from your friends and give it to the food bank.
3. Find the restaurant review section of a local newspaper. Read the reviews and choose a restaurant that interests you. Go to the restaurant and order a meal. Do you agree or disagree with the person who reviewed the restaurant you visited? Write your own review of the restaurant.

Love

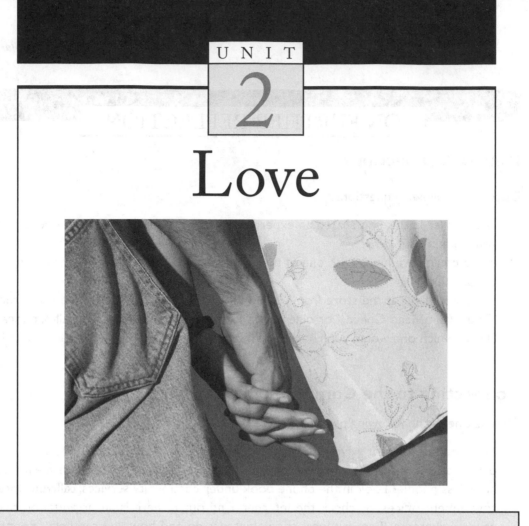

*H*ave you ever been in love? How do you decide who to date or, eventually, to marry? Would you date or marry someone from another culture?

The writers in this unit explore these and other questions about love. First, poet Gary Soto remembers the first time he walked with a girl. Next, Harvey Price, a young American working in Thailand, recalls his experience dating a Thai. Then poet John Agard compares love to the wind, river, and sea. Finally, writer Longhang Nguyen recalls when her sister had to choose between two very different men.

There is a popular song called "What Is This Thing Called Love?" You may not find the answer here, but you will get four very distinctive points of view.

Oranges

SETTING THE CONTEXT

Discussion

Discuss the following questions as a class.

1. In your country, are boys and girls allowed to date? If so, at what age do they start dating?
2. What activities do boys and girls typically do on a date in your country?
3. How do boys and girls show that they like each other?

READING THE POEM

As you read the poem, think about the title. Why do you think the poet called it "Oranges"?

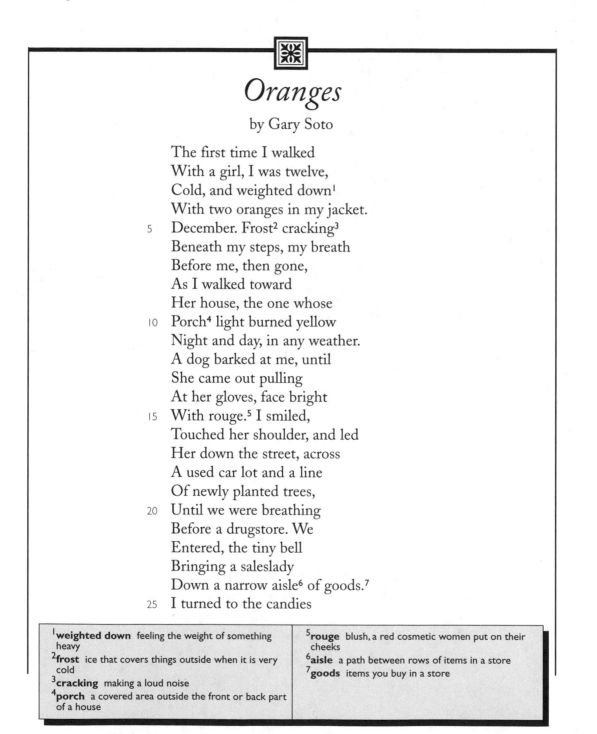

Oranges

by Gary Soto

The first time I walked
With a girl, I was twelve,
Cold, and weighted down[1]
With two oranges in my jacket.
5   December. Frost[2] cracking[3]
Beneath my steps, my breath
Before me, then gone,
As I walked toward
Her house, the one whose
10   Porch[4] light burned yellow
Night and day, in any weather.
A dog barked at me, until
She came out pulling
At her gloves, face bright
15   With rouge.[5] I smiled,
Touched her shoulder, and led
Her down the street, across
A used car lot and a line
Of newly planted trees,
20   Until we were breathing
Before a drugstore. We
Entered, the tiny bell
Bringing a saleslady
Down a narrow aisle[6] of goods.[7]
25   I turned to the candies

[1] **weighted down** feeling the weight of something heavy
[2] **frost** ice that covers things outside when it is very cold
[3] **cracking** making a loud noise
[4] **porch** a covered area outside the front or back part of a house

[5] **rouge** blush, a red cosmetic women put on their cheeks
[6] **aisle** a path between rows of items in a store
[7] **goods** items you buy in a store

Tiered[8] like bleachers,[9]
And asked what she wanted—
Light in her eyes, a smile
Starting at the corners
30 Of her mouth. I fingered
A nickel[10] in my pocket,
And when she lifted a chocolate
That cost a dime,[11]
I didn't say anything.
35 I took the nickel from
My pocket, then an orange,
And set them quietly on
The counter. When I looked up,
The lady's eyes met mine,
40 And held them, knowing
Very well what it was all
About.

Outside,
A few cars hissing past,
45 Fog hanging like old
Coats between the trees.
I took my girl's hand
In mine for two blocks,
Then released it to let
50 Her unwrap the chocolate.
I peeled my orange
That was so bright against
The gray of December
That, from a distance
55 Someone might have thought
I was making a fire in my hands.

---

[8]**tiered** arranged in steps and rows, one above the other
[9]**bleachers** seats for people watching sports outside
[10]**nickel** a coin in the United States and Canada worth five cents
[11]**dime** a coin in the United States and Canada worth ten cents

THINKING ABOUT THE POEM

Comprehension

Discuss the following questions as a class.

1. What was in the boy's jacket? What do you think he wanted to do with them?
2. Why do you think the girl was wearing rouge on her face? Do girls this age ever wear rouge in your country? If so, when?
3. Where did the boy and the girl go? Why?
4. How do you think the girl felt when the boy asked her what she wanted? How do you know?
5. How did the boy pay the saleslady for the chocolate? Why do you think she accepted his payment?
6. Do you think the boy liked the girl? Support your answer with examples from the poem.
7. Do you think the girl liked the boy? Support your answer with examples from the poem.
8. Why do you think Gary Soto named this poem "Oranges"?

Focus on Reading: Pronoun Referents

Pronouns take the place of nouns. Writers use pronouns for variety, so they don't have to repeat the same nouns too often. When you read, it is important to identify the *pronoun referents*, or the nouns the pronouns refer to. You can identify them by looking at the preceding lines. For example, look at the boldfaced pronouns in lines 8–11 of "Oranges":

> *As I walked toward*
> **Her** *house, the* **one** *whose*
> *Porch light burned yellow*
> *Night and day, in any weather.*

The pronoun *her* refers to the girl, and *one* refers to the girl's house.

A. Read the poem again. Write the referent for each pronoun on the line.

1. She (line 13) _____

2. we (line 20) _____

3. she (line 27) _____

4. them (line 37) _____

5. them (line 40) _____

6. it (line 49) _____

B. The pronoun *it* in line 41 does not have a specific referent. In this case, *it* refers to an understanding between the saleslady and the boy. What do the saleslady and the boy both understand?

Focus on Literature: Sensory Images

Poets often use *sensory images* so that the reader can see, hear, touch, taste, and smell what is happening in the poem. For example, look at lines 5–7 of "Oranges":

> *December. Frost cracking*
> *Beneath my steps, my breath*
> *Before me, then gone*

The images allow the reader to hear the boy's steps as he walks on the frozen ground and to see his breath in the cold winter air.

A. Read the poem again. Use the chart to list sensory images that allow you to see, hear, touch, taste, and smell things. Then compare charts in small groups.

See	Hear	Touch/Feel	Taste	Smell
My breath before me	*Frost cracking*			

B. Discuss the following questions as a class.
1. Reread lines 45–46. What two things does the poet compare in this simile? How do the sensory images help you see and feel the weather?
2. What other sensory images describe the weather?
3. Reread lines 51–56 of the poem. How does the image of the orange help describe the weather?
4. What does the image *a fire in my hands* refer to?

Expansion

Discuss the following questions in small groups.

1. The boy didn't have enough money to pay for the chocolate. Have you ever been in a similar situation? What did you do?
2. When the saleslady's eyes met the boy's eyes, they reached a silent understanding. Has anything like this ever happened to you? If so, tell the class about it.

RESPONDING TO THE POEM

Write about one of the following topics.

1. **Going Out Together.** Write a poem about a time you went out with a boy, girl, or group of friends. Use "Oranges" as a model. Use sensory images to help the reader see, hear, touch, taste, and smell what you are describing. Use the following steps and your own ideas.

   • List as many sensory images as you can recall about the experience. Write them in the chart. Use the chart on page 39 as a model.

See	Hear	Touch/Feel	Taste	Smell

   • Write the poem. Include sensory images from your chart.
   • Choose the image that best describes the experience or your feeling about it. Use this image as the title of your poem.

2. **The First Time.** Gary Soto was twelve the first time he walked with a girl. The experience was special, so he wrote a poem about it. Think about how old you were the first time you did something special (for example, went on a date, rode a bicycle, went to school). Write a poem, paragraph, or essay about this experience. Use sensory images to describe what you were doing and feeling, where you were, who you were with, and why the experience was special.

3. **Paying for Something.** In the poem, the boy didn't have enough money to buy chocolate for the girl. Have you ever been in a similar situation? If so, write a story about the experience.

Peer Response

Work with a partner. Exchange papers and read each other's writing. Discuss the following questions.

- Does the writer use any pronouns? If so, what nouns do the pronouns refer to?
- What sensory images does the writer use? Which do you like best?
- Do you have any questions for the writer?
- What do you like best about the writing?

After you discuss your ideas, you may want to revise your writing.

About the Author

Gary Soto was born in Fresno, California in 1952. He writes poetry, essays, plays, and short stories. He has published many collections of poems, including *Living up the Street*, *Black Hair*, and *A Fire in My Hands*. He teaches at the University of California at Berkeley.

I Date a Thai

SETTING THE CONTEXT

Discussion

Discuss the following questions as a class.

1. In your country, do young men and women usually go out in couples or in groups? Do men usually invite women on dates? Do women invite men?

2. Does a chaperone (an older person responsible for young people on social occasions) ever go with the couple or group?

3. Have you ever dated someone from another culture? Would you consider doing so? Why or why not?

Vocabulary

The boldfaced words in the following sentences are from the story on pages 43–44. Use the context to guess the meanings of the boldfaced words. Use a dictionary if necessary. Then match the boldfaced words with the correct definitions that follow. Compare your answers in small groups.

_____ 1. John asked Susan on a date. Their **rendezvous** was Gino's restaurant.

_____ 2. My friend **assured** me he would return my CD, so I lent it to him.

_____ 3. Once we **established** the rules, it was easy to play the game.

_____ 4. I **climbed aboard** the train in Chicago. Two days later, I was in Los Angeles.

_____ 5. As we **approached** the city, the traffic became heavier and heavier.

_____ 6. I haven't read the assignment carefully; I only **glanced** at it.

a. decided on
b. got on
c. looked quickly
d. moved closer to
e. meeting place
f. promised

READING THE STORY

Think about the title. What do you think the story will be about? After you read, think about the title again. Was your prediction correct?

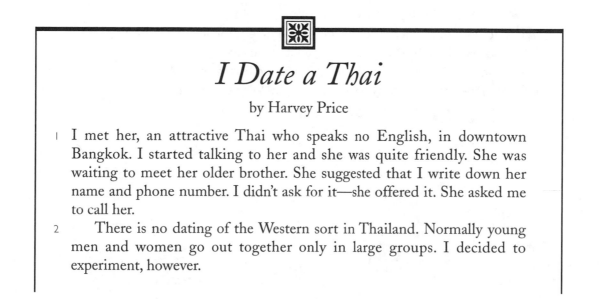

I Date a Thai

by Harvey Price

1   I met her, an attractive Thai who speaks no English, in downtown Bangkok. I started talking to her and she was quite friendly. She was waiting to meet her older brother. She suggested that I write down her name and phone number. I didn't ask for it—she offered it. She asked me to call her.

2   There is no dating of the Western sort in Thailand. Normally young men and women go out together only in large groups. I decided to experiment, however.

3   A few days later I called and asked her out. She asked me if I was going to bring anyone with me. When I replied no, she seemed pleased.

4   She said she would come alone also. She told me not to tell anyone I was meeting her. Our rendezvous was to be in the lobby of a theater. The date was for 6 P.M.

5   I arrived at the theater a little early. At 6 P.M. she arrived. She immediately asked me if I had told anyone about our meeting. I assured her I had not.

6   Having established the complete secrecy of our date, we then proceeded out of the lobby, into the street. I followed her, having no idea where she was taking me.

7   We walked about a block, and then she said we should take a bus. I agreed, and we climbed aboard. We rode for about 15 minutes, then got off the bus and continued walking. I still had no idea where she was taking me.

8   It was then we approached a yellow bus.

9   "This will take you home," she said. "It's starting to get dark. I have to get home before my older brother . . . Goodbye . . . Thank you."

10   In a state of confusion, I got on the yellow bus. I glanced at my watch. It was 6:20 P.M.

THINKING ABOUT THE STORY

Comprehension

Discuss the following questions as a class.

1. Retell the events in the story. Use your own words.
2. What do you think the author expected the date to be like?
3. What do you think the woman expected it to be like?
4. Which person do you think was most surprised by the date? Why?
5. Do you think they will meet each other again? Why or why not?

Focus on Reading: Quoted and Reported Speech

When including conversation in a story, writers use *quoted speech* and *reported speech*.

Quoted speech reports the speaker's exact words. Writers use quotation marks to identify quoted speech. For example, look at paragraph 9 of "I Date a Thai":

> *"This will take you home," she said.*

Reported speech does not give the speaker's exact words, so writers do not use quotation marks to identify them. For example, look at paragraph 4:

> *She said she would come alone also.*

A. Reread the story. Answer the following questions.

1. Underline all the examples of quoted speech once. Count the examples.
2. Underline all the examples of reported speech twice. Count the examples.
3. Does the author use more quoted speech or reported speech? Why do you think he does this?

B. Study the examples of quoted and reported speech in the box. Then change the examples of reported speech on the next page to quoted speech. Be sure to use correct punctuation and to make any necessary pronoun and verb changes. (**Note:** More than one answer is possible.) Discuss your answers as a class.

Quoted Speech	Reported Speech
*"**I listen** to music every day," he said.*	*He said **he listened** to music every day.*
*"**Are you** going to bring a friend?" she asked.*	*She asked **if I was** going to bring a friend.*
*"**I will** meet **you** at three o'clock," I said.*	*I said I **would** meet **her** at three o'clock.*
*"**Don't** tell anyone **I'm** going," he said.*	*He told **her not to** tell anyone **he was** going.*
*"**Have you** told anyone about the the party?" I asked.*	*I asked **if he had** told anyone about the party.*

1. She asked me to call her.

   "Call me," she said. _____

2. She asked me if I was going to bring anyone with me.

   _____

3. She said she would come alone also.

   _____

4. She told me not to tell anyone I was meeting her.

   _____

5. She immediately asked me if I had told anyone about our meeting.

   _____

Focus on Literature: Verbal Irony

> Writers sometimes use words to say the opposite of what they mean. This is called *verbal irony*. For example, American writer Stephen Crane (1871–1900) wrote a poem about the cruelty of war. He called the poem "War Is Kind." The title "War Is Kind" is ironic because its meaning is the opposite of the meaning of the poem itself—that war is violent and terrible. Crane's ironic title surprises readers and makes them think more deeply about the nature and consequences of war.

Discuss the following questions as a class.

1. What does the title "I Date a Thai" suggest the story will be about?
2. Did the story surprise you? If so, how?
3. How is the title ironic?

Expansion

Discuss the following questions in small groups.

1. Do you like the title of the story? Why or why not?
2. Have you ever had a surprising or unusual date? If so, describe it.
3. Have you ever lived or traveled in a different culture? If so, did anything about the customs surprise you? Explain.

RESPONDING TO THE STORY

Write about one of the following topics.

1. **A Surprising Experience.** Write about a date or other experience that ended differently than expected. Use the following questions to help you.

   - What did you expect to happen?
   - What happened in the end?
   - How did you feel?
   - What did you do after it happened?
   - What did you learn?

2. **Point of View.** "I Date a Thai" is told from Harvey Price's point of view. He is the first-person narrator (or *I*) in the story. Imagine that you are the Thai woman. Retell the story from her point of view, so that she is the first-person narrator (or *I*) in the story. You can begin the story like this: "I met him, a tall, attractive American who spoke Thai, in . . . "

3. **An Ideal Date.** Imagine that you could go on a date with any man or woman. Write a paragraph or essay about the date. Use the following questions to help you.

   - Who would you choose?
   - Where would you go?
   - What would you do?

Peer Response

Work with a partner. Exchange papers and read each other's writing. Discuss the following questions.

- Does the writer use any quoted speech?
- Does the writer use any reported speech?
- Are there any examples of irony?
- Do you have any questions for the writer?
- What do you like best about the writing?

After you discuss your ideas, you may want to revise your writing.

About the Author

Harvey Price taught law and accounting at Chulalongkorn University in Thailand from 1962 to 1963. He was a volunteer for the Peace Corps, a U.S. government program that sends teachers, engineers, health workers, and other professionals to work in developing countries. "I Date a Thai" is from a collection of stories called *The Peace Corps Reader*.

Wind and River Romance

SETTING THE CONTEXT

Discussion

Discuss the following questions as a class.

1. What are the two people in the picture doing?
2. What things in nature do you see in the picture?
3. How do you think the people and things are related?

READING THE POEM

"Wind and River Romance" is written in a nonstandard variety of English typical of parts of the Caribbean. As you read the poem, notice some differences between this variety of English and standard English. Also, think about how the poet makes the Wind, River, and Sea seem human.

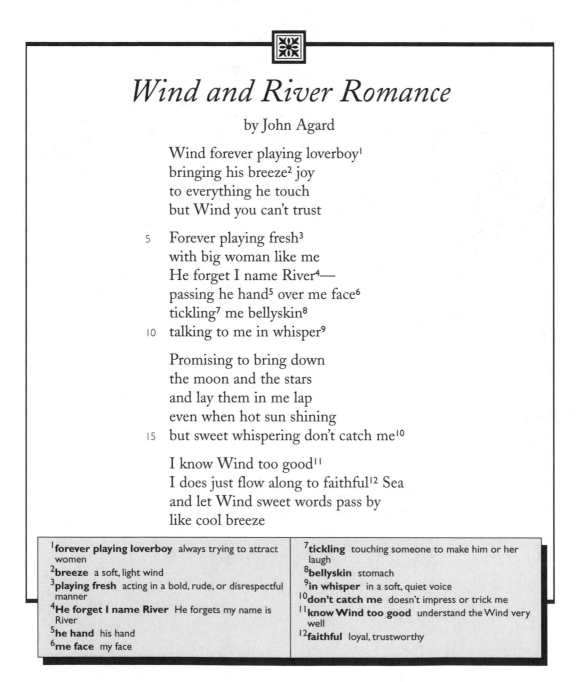

Wind and River Romance

by John Agard

Wind forever playing loverboy[1]
bringing his breeze[2] joy
to everything he touch
but Wind you can't trust

5   Forever playing fresh[3]
with big woman like me
He forget I name River[4]—
passing he hand[5] over me face[6]
tickling[7] me bellyskin[8]
10 talking to me in whisper[9]

Promising to bring down
the moon and the stars
and lay them in me lap
even when hot sun shining
15 but sweet whispering don't catch me[10]

I know Wind too good[11]
I does just flow along to faithful[12] Sea
and let Wind sweet words pass by
like cool breeze

[1] **forever playing loverboy** always trying to attract women
[2] **breeze** a soft, light wind
[3] **playing fresh** acting in a bold, rude, or disrespectful manner
[4] **He forget I name River** He forgets my name is River
[5] **he hand** his hand
[6] **me face** my face
[7] **tickling** touching someone to make him or her laugh
[8] **bellyskin** stomach
[9] **in whisper** in a soft, quiet voice
[10] **don't catch me** doesn't impress or trick me
[11] **know Wind too good** understand the Wind very well
[12] **faithful** loyal, trustworthy

THINKING ABOUT THE POEM

Comprehension

A. Read the following statements. Write *T* if you think the statement is *True*. Write *F* if you think it is *False*. Then compare your answers in small groups.

_____ 1. The Wind is in love with the River.

_____ 2. The River is in love with the Wind.

_____ 3. The Wind always tells the truth.

_____ 4. The Wind likes to make promises.

_____ 5. The Wind has a sweet and kind way of talking.

_____ 6. The Wind can make people feel good.

_____ 7. The Sea is honest and dependable.

_____ 8. The River believes what the Wind tells her.

_____ 9. The Wind thinks he is a great lover.

_____ 10. The River will go with the Wind.

B. Discuss the following questions as a class.

1. Who is telling the story in the poem?
2. What does the Wind promise the River? What does he mean by this?
3. Why does the River choose the Sea instead of the Wind?
4. How do you think the Wind would define love? Why?
5. How do you think the River would define love? Why?

Focus on Reading: Making Prose Sense of a Poem

Sometimes you can better understand the meaning of a poem by making prose sense of it—that is, by rewriting the poem using conventional writing rules. This is especially true for poetry that is written in nonstandard English. For example, lines 1–4 of "Wind and River Romance" can be rewritten in prose as follows:

The Wind is always trying to attract women. He is always traveling around and making women feel happy, but you can't trust him.

Changing some words and adding punctuation to make complete sentences can help you clarify the meaning of the poem.

A. Rewrite lines 5–20 of "Wind and River Romance" as prose. Change words and add punctuation marks to make complete sentences.

B. Compare your prose versions of the poem in small groups. Discuss the following questions.

1. Did rewriting the poem as prose help you understand its meaning?
2. Which prose version do you like best? Why?
3. Which do you like better—the prose version or the poem? Why?

Focus on Literature: Personification

> Sometimes writers describe a thing or quality as if it were a person. This is called *personification*. In "Wind and River Romance," John Agard personifies the Wind, River, and Sea: He describes them as people, with human qualities. For example, in the first line he says the Wind is "forever playing loverboy."

How does John Agard personify the Wind, River, and Sea? Write the following human qualities in the correct column of the chart.

plays loverboy   is a big woman   whispers sweetly
can't be trusted   is faithful   brings others joy
is not fooled or tricked talks fresh   tickles others

Wind	River	Sea
plays loverboy		

Expansion

Discuss the following questions in small groups.

1. Do you think the Wind and River could ever have a love relationship? Explain.
2. Is your definition of love similar to the Wind's? The River's? Something else? Explain.
3. There are many English words and expressions that describe a man who enjoys the company of many women. They include *loverboy*, *ladies' man*, *playboy*, *Don Juan*, and *Casanova*. (**Note:** *Don Juan* and *Casanova* are the names of characters from literature.) Are there any expressions in your native language that describe this kind of man? If so, what are they?

RESPONDING TO THE POEM

Write about one of the following topics.

1. **X and Y Romance.** Using "Wind and River Romance" as a model, write a poem about love. Include natural elements or other nonhuman characters, and use personification to give them positive and negative human qualities. For example, you might compare love to different kinds of food. Or you might consider how love compares—positively or negatively—to other aspects of nature (for example, earthquakes, fire).

2. **Love Letter from the Wind.** Imagine that you are the Wind. Write the River a love letter. Explain that you have many good qualities, and try to persuade her to go out with you.

3. **Letter from the River.** Imagine that you are the River. Write a letter to the Wind, telling him what you think of him. You can be gentle and polite, thanking the Wind for his attention but explaining why you are not interested. Or, you can be direct and forceful, telling him that you don't believe anything he says and to leave you alone.

Peer Response

Work with a partner. Exchange papers and read each other's writing. Discuss the following questions.

- Is the writing in poetry or prose form?
- Are there any examples of personification?
- How do you think the writer defines love? Why?
- Do you have any questions for the writer?
- What do you like best about the writing?

After you discuss your ideas, you may want to revise your writing.

About the Poet

John Agard is from Guyana. In addition to writing poetry for adults and children, he has worked as an actor and a performer with a jazz group. In 1982, he won the Cuban Casa de las Americas poetry prize for his collection of poems *Man to Pan*. "Wind and River Romance" is from an anthology of Caribbean poetry called *Caribbean Poetry Now*.

Rain Music

SETTING THE CONTEXT

Discussion

What qualities are most important to you in choosing a husband or wife? Rank the following qualities from 1 (most important) to 10 (least important). Compare your answers in small groups.

_____ similar cultural or religious background

_____ similar interests

_____ parental approval

_____ sense of humor

_____ intelligence

_____ attractiveness

_____ kindness

_____ wealth

_____ honesty

_____ good job

Vocabulary

The boldfaced words in the following sentences are from the story on pages 56–59. Use the context to guess the meanings of the boldfaced words. Use a dictionary if necessary. Then match the boldfaced words with the correct definitions that follow. Compare your answers in small groups.

_____ 1. Our team won the basketball game, **finishing off** the other team 81 to 68.

_____ 2. Sometimes children **pout** or cry when they don't get what they want.

_____ 3. We called the police when someone started **assaulting** our neighbor.

_____ 4. I lost my research notes, so I had to go back to the library and **start over** again.

_____ 5. Julia felt angry when she learned that her friend was **using her** for her car.

_____ 6. Many busy parents don't spend much **quality time** with their children.

_____ 7. After months of fighting, the two armies agreed to a **truce**.

_____ 8. Every winter, my grandfather **trudged** through miles of snow on his way to school.

_____ 9. The cows are **penned in** with a fence so that they can't escape.

_____10. The hikers **lugged** their heavy backpacks up the mountain.

_____11. Walking and driving are two good ways to get to the library. However, **the latter** is better if you are going to borrow a lot of heavy books.

_____12. Some people think the desert is hot all the time. **In actuality**, night temperatures there are very low.

a. begin again
b. fighting, attacking
c. what is a fact
d. carried something heavy with difficulty
e. making someone do what you want in an unfair way
f. defeating
g. the second thing in a series of two things
h. kept inside an enclosed area
i. push out one's lower lip to show sadness
j. walked with slow, heavy steps
k. temporary peace
l. time spent giving someone your complete attention

READING THE STORY

As you read the story, think about the title. How is it related to the story?

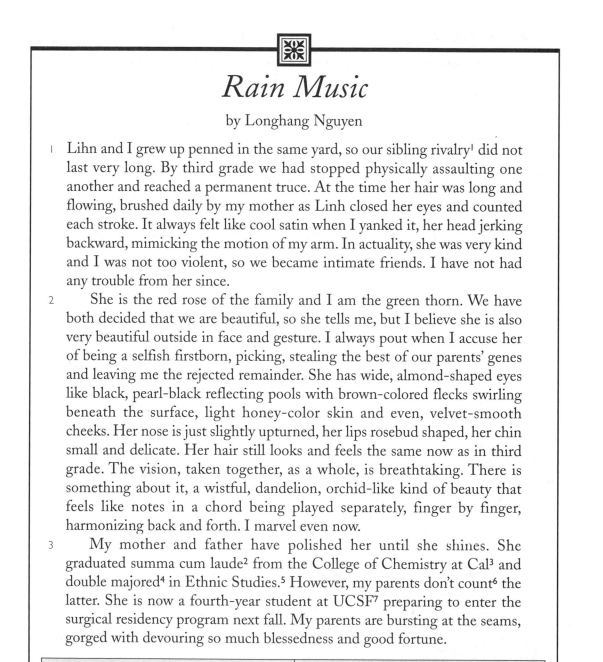

Rain Music

by Longhang Nguyen

1   Lihn and I grew up penned in the same yard, so our sibling rivalry[1] did not last very long. By third grade we had stopped physically assaulting one another and reached a permanent truce. At the time her hair was long and flowing, brushed daily by my mother as Linh closed her eyes and counted each stroke. It always felt like cool satin when I yanked it, her head jerking backward, mimicking the motion of my arm. In actuality, she was very kind and I was not too violent, so we became intimate friends. I have not had any trouble from her since.

2   She is the red rose of the family and I am the green thorn. We have both decided that we are beautiful, so she tells me, but I believe she is also very beautiful outside in face and gesture. I always pout when I accuse her of being a selfish firstborn, picking, stealing the best of our parents' genes and leaving me the rejected remainder. She has wide, almond-shaped eyes like black, pearl-black reflecting pools with brown-colored flecks swirling beneath the surface, light honey-color skin and even, velvet-smooth cheeks. Her nose is just slightly upturned, her lips rosebud shaped, her chin small and delicate. Her hair still looks and feels the same now as in third grade. The vision, taken together, as a whole, is breathtaking. There is something about it, a wistful, dandelion, orchid-like kind of beauty that feels like notes in a chord being played separately, finger by finger, harmonizing back and forth. I marvel even now.

3   My mother and father have polished her until she shines. She graduated summa cum laude[2] from the College of Chemistry at Cal[3] and double majored[4] in Ethnic Studies.[5] However, my parents don't count[6] the latter. She is now a fourth-year student at UCSF[7] preparing to enter the surgical residency program next fall. My parents are bursting at the seams, gorged with devouring so much blessedness and good fortune.

---

[1]**sibling rivalry** competition between brothers and sisters for parents' attention
[2]**summa cum laude** the highest honors given to American college students when they graduate
[3]**Cal** University of California, Berkeley

[4]**double majored** majored in two subjects
[5]**Ethnic Studies** a college program offering courses in the history and culture of different ethnic groups
[6]**don't count** don't consider something important
[7]**UCSF** University of California, San Francisco

4   "Will your daughter become a surgeon?" our relatives ask.

5   "It's possible," my father says, beaming.[8]

6   "She is friends with this young man in her class. He's tall, distinguished-looking, loyal and respectful to his parents, hard-working but generous. He was even born in Vietnam! But he came over here with his family in 1975. He went to Harvard"[9]—my mother pauses to let the relatives gasp in unison—"on a full scholarship!" She smiles modestly, then lowers her eyes.

7   "A possible son-in-law?" they ask.

8   She shrugs and sighs. "That is up to God."

9   Linh hasn't told my parents about David. She met him five years ago during her final year at Cal. That semester they were in three classes together: a choral class, an Afro-American literature class, and a creative writing class. They became good friends.

10   David is a writer. His subjects are ordinary preoccupations of other writers: his mother, the father he has never seen or known, the friends of his childhood. Some of them are dead now. The others are spread out across the country. One is a construction worker in St. Louis. Another is a teacher in Baton Rouge. The third is a journalist in Washington, D.C. They write to him once in a while or call him. Lihn hasn't met any of them, but she knows them all.

11   After David feverishly completes a story, Lihn cooks him dinner. Afterward, she tucks him into bed and sits nearby in the wicker chair, legs drawn up and hugged tightly to her chest, to watch him while he sleeps. His soft, black curls rest against the white of the pillow, his closed eyelids flutter minutely while he dreams, his breath whistles through the evenness of his teeth as the cover grazes the dark honey of his skin.

12   They always have a good time together, and he makes her laugh in many different ways, wherever they happen to be. He always gets close to finishing her off during a tennis set, but then she cries out that he has cheated and treated her unfairly and he has to start over again. He never wins. Sometimes they sing together, his clear, resonant tenor melding with her flutelike, crystalline soprano. Then they have tea.

13   I know all about David. She won't stop talking about him, but I know less about Thanh, the Vietnamese friend at UCSF. I know he's nice but that's all. She woke me up this morning at ten thirty and said, "It's a bright, beautiful, Saturday morning. Let's go and have a picnic."

---

[8]**beaming** smiling happily

[9]**Harvard** the oldest and probably most famous American university

14   "No, no," I mumbled hazily in my sleep. "Take David. Leave me alone."

15   "I don't want to take David. I want to spend quality time with you, my darling sister. Get up, you piece of mutton. Toast on the table in five minutes and we're leaving in half an hour."

16   "Oh, lord," I groaned "I'm being punished for sins from past lives."

17   We arrived at the park at twelve, lugged our ample picnic hamper[10] heavily laden with cheese, fruits, sandwiches, ice, and bottles of juice from the car, and trudged into the heart of the lightly shaded, green forest. When I opened the basket and took out the butter, she started to talk.

18   "David kissed me last night . . ."

19   "He what?"

20   " . . . or I kissed him. It just happened, I guess. He invited me to dinner, promised to cook a sumptuous Cajun[11] feast with Vietnamese desserts. *Bánh flanc*, you know. My favorite." She plucked a blade of grass from its roots and twisted it back and forth, watching a streak of feeble, yellow sun play on its linear edges. "I expected it to be a celebration. He's just finished his first novel, not quite a love story, he says, and he wanted me to read it." She spoke more softly. "When I arrived, he had set tiny blossoms in water dishes throughout the apartment. It smelled wonderful. The food was delicious, everything so lovely, so tranquil[12] I didn't know where to begin. After dinner he led me into the living room.

21   "'Rain music,' he said. 'It's for you.' After the last note on the piano had stopped to echo, he turned toward me and kissed me for a long, long time. I didn't know what I was doing. I just couldn't stop. I didn't breathe. When he let me go, I kept thinking of his hands and fingers, seeing them fly over the ivory keys like little Russian men dancing in their black fur hats and noticing how his brown was different from mine. I was raging[13] inside, screaming in my head, 'Why can't his fingers be brown like mine, be my brown? Why is his hair curly, not straight like mine?' I saw brown pigments[14] run across my eyes, all different colored browns. Those pigments keep us apart. How do I stand there and tell this man who writes me music and whose hands burn my cheeks that I can't be who he wants me to be?"

22   "But he doesn't want to change you."

---

[10]**hamper** a basket used for carrying food
[11]**Cajun** related to a style of spicy cooking created by French-speaking immigrants to Louisiana
[12]**tranquil** calm, peaceful
[13]**raging** experiencing very strong feelings
[14]**pigment** natural substance that colors hair, skin, etc.

23   "No, I can't be who he thinks I am. He's a damned starving writer.[15] He can't give me anything, just himself. And he doesn't even know that I'm using him. Damn it! He doesn't even know." She choked on her tears, swallowed, and cried quietly, hugging her knees, until exhausted. The leaves rustled softly while I waited.

24   After a while she grew calm, her eyes gazing steadily at the flashing water of the stream below. "I love Thanh. I would never hurt him for anything. Throughout the four years at UCSF, he has been so patient, so kind, so dedicated to medicine for its own good, not just for its technology, even though he's brilliant and understands these details completely. He's so perfect for me, just perfect. It's like he stepped out of my story and came to life. We speak the same language and share the same past. Everything. And Mom and Dad, they've done so much for us. Now they think they've won the lottery from God for being good all their life."

25   "But how do you feel about Thanh? How does he make you feel?"

26   "He will be my lifelong friend. He'll make a wonderful father. That's what a husband should be. Our children will know the culture and customs of our homeland. They'll speak Vietnamese and English, just like us."

27   "And how does David make you feel?" I tugged at her gently.

28   She bowed her head for a long while reflecting. Then she softly murmured, "It's just not possible."

29   "But why? I don't understand."

30   The picnic basket remained quite full. Neither of us was hungry. It threatened to rain as we packed up to go home. On the drive back, we were silent. I watched the windshield wipers swing back and forth, clearing rain cascading down the front window.

---

[15]**starving writer** a creative person, such as a writer, who can't earn enough money to buy food (also **starving artist**)

THINKING ABOUT THE STORY

Comprehension

Discuss the following questions as a class.

1. How are the author and Linh related?
2. How does Linh know David? What kind of relationship do they have?
3. How does Linh know Thanh? What kind of relationship do they have?
4. Why do you think Linh's parents know about Thanh but not David?
5. Why do you think Linh tells her sister about David?
6. Who do Linh's parents hope she will marry? Why?
7. Who does Linh choose in the end? Why?
8. How does the title relate to the story?

Focus on Reading: Making Inferences

Sometimes writers don't state information directly; they only imply or suggest it. In this case, we have to draw our own conclusions, or *make inferences* about what they mean. For example, in paragraph 3 of "Rain Music," Longhang Nguyen writes:

> She [Linh] graduated summa cum laude from the College of Chemistry at Cal and double majored in Ethnic Studies. However, my parents don't count the latter.

The author states directly that Linh graduated with highest honors from Cal and majored in Chemistry and Ethnic Studies. She also implies that her parents think Chemistry is more useful than Ethnic Studies. We can infer this because she tells us that they *don't count* Ethnic Studies.

A. Read the following sentences. Write *S* if the information is stated directly in the story. Write *I* if it is implied. Underline information in the story that helped you infer the *I* answers. Then compare answers in small groups.

_____ 1. Linh's parents like Thanh.

_____ 2. Thanh and Linh are classmates at UCSF.

_____ 3. Linh hasn't told her parents about David.

_____ 4. Linh's parents wouldn't like David.

_____ 5. Linh likes David because he is different from her.

_____ 6. Linh and Thanh are of the same race and culture.

_____ 7. David plays the piano.

_____ 8. David doesn't have much money.

_____ 9. Linh is attracted to David.

_____ 10. Linh isn't attracted to Thanh.

B. Reread this conversation between the author and Linh. Then discuss the questions that follow as a class.

> "And how does David make you feel?" I tugged at her gently.
> She bowed her head for a long while reflecting. Then she softly murmured, "It's just not possible."
> "But why? I don't understand."

1. What can you infer about Linh's beliefs about love and marriage?
2. What can you infer about the author's beliefs?
3. Why can't the author understand Linh's answer?

Focus on Literature: Similes and Metaphors

Remember that writers sometimes use *similes* and *metaphors* to create strong images. Similes make comparisons using *like* or *as*. For example:

*Her skin was **as** white **as** snow.*

*My love is **like** a red, red rose.*

Metaphors make comparisons without using *like* or *as*. For example:

*She has a **heart** of **gold**.*

*We make many friends on the **road** of **life**.*

A. Read the following sentences from "Rain Music." Write the two things that the author is comparing. Then circle *S* if the sentence contains a simile and *M* if it contains a metaphor. Compare answers in small groups.

1. Her hair always felt like cool satin when I yanked it.

    Her _____ is compared to _____.   **S**   **M**

2. She is the red rose of the family and I am the green thorn.

    a. _____ is compared to a _____ .   S   M

    b. _____ is compared to a _____ .   S   M

3. She has wide, almond-shaped eyes like black, pearl-black reflecting pools.

    Her _____ are compared to _____ .   S   M

4. She has light honey-color skin.

    Her _____ is compared to _____ .   S   M

5. Her lips are rosebud shaped.

    Her _____ are compared to a _____ .   S   M

B. Find and underline two other similes or metaphors in the story. Discuss their meanings with a partner.

Expansion

A. Use the following Venn diagram to show the similarities and differences between David and Thanh. Write the qualities that only David has in the left part of the diagram. Write the qualities that only Thanh has in the right part of the diagram. Write the qualities that both David and Thanh have in the middle of the diagram. Then compare diagrams in small groups.

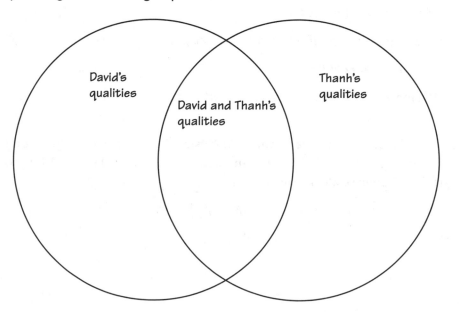

B. Work with a partner. List the similarities between Linh and David in the left column of the chart. List the similarities between Linh and Thanh in the right column of the chart. Use information from the Venn diagram to help you. Then compare your charts as a class.

Similarities between Linh and David	Similarities between Linh and Thanh

C. Discuss the following questions in small groups.

1. Why do you think David was attracted to Linh?
2. Why do you think Linh was attracted to David?
3. What do you think is more important in a relationship—similarities or differences? Explain.

RESPONDING TO THE STORY

Write about one of the following topics.

1. **A Different Ending.** Do you think the story could have ended differently? If so, how? Write another ending for "Rain Music." If you like, you can begin after Linh says, "How do I stand there and tell this man who writes me music and whose hands burn my cheeks that I can't be who he wants me to be?"

2. **Parental Expectations.** In "Rain Music," the author implies what her parents' expectations are for her and her sister. Write a paragraph or essay about your parents' expectations for you. Use the following questions to help you.

   • What expectations do/did your parents have for you?
   • How have these expectations influenced your life?
   • Do you share your parents' expectations for you? Explain.
   • If your expectations differ from those of your parents, has this affected your relationship? If so, how?

3. **Using Someone.** Linh confides that she's been "using David." Do you think it is ever acceptable to use another person? If so, when? Choose one of the following opinion statements (or write a different opinion statement). Write a paragraph or essay, supporting your opinion statement with examples from your life.

- It's acceptable to use people in any situation to get something you want. Life is about competing and winning.
- It's acceptable to use another person to get something you want if no one gets hurt.
- Everyone uses people in some ways—to learn something or to get something, such as a job. This is acceptable if everyone knows what's happening and agrees to it.
- It's never acceptable to use another person. You should always earn everything yourself, through your own efforts.

Peer Response

Work with a partner. Exchange papers and read each other's writing. Discuss the following questions.

- Does the writer state an opinion? If so, what is it?
- Can you make any inferences from information in the writing? If so, what are they? What information led you to your conclusions?
- Do you have any questions for the writer?
- What do you like best about the writing?

After you discuss your ideas, you may want to revise your writing.

About the Author

Longhang Nguyen was born in Vietnam. She immigrated to the United States in 1979 and lives in California. Her story "Rain Music" is from the short-story collection *American Dragons: Twenty-Five Asian American Voices*.

ON FURTHER REFLECTION

Making Connections

Discuss the following topics.

1. In both "I Date a Thai" and "Rain Music," a main character dates someone from another race and culture. Do you think either or both characters should continue the relationship? Why or why not?
2. Which character in the readings from this unit do you find the most romantic? The least romantic? Explain.
3. If you could go on a date with any character from the readings in this unit, who would you choose? Why?

Connecting to the Community

Choose one of the following projects.

1. Write a letter, card, or e-mail message to someone you love or like very much. Write about what you've been doing and ask about what he or she is doing.
2. Where are the best places to go for a date in your city or town? In small groups, make a list of the "Top 5 Places for a Date." Explain your choices and the reasons for them.
3. Does your local newspaper have a Personals section—a section where single people advertise for a date? If so, bring the section to class and discuss it. Do you like any of the ads? If so, which ones? What are the advantages of placing an ad in the Personals section? What are the disadvantages? Would you ever place an ad? Why or why not?

3

Clothes

What do your clothes say about you? Do you choose clothes to be part of a group or to express your individuality?

The clothes people wear—and what they might mean to them and others—is the topic explored by the writers in this unit. First, poet Pablo Neruda sings a song in praise of a pair of socks he received as a gift. Writer Maya Angelou gives her reflections on fashion and personal identity. Then, poet Dana Naone shows the powerful effect of a young woman's skirt as she walks by some young men. Finally, playwright John Patrick Shanley explores the feelings a red coat inspires in a teenaged boy and girl.

Whether you care a little or a lot about what you wear, your clothes are a part of who you are. And, like your gestures and body language, your clothes give other people information about you. Just ask the characters you meet in this unit.

Ode to My Socks

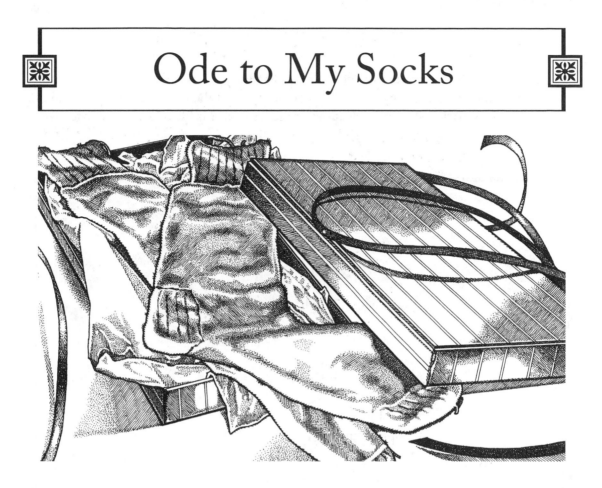

SETTING THE CONTEXT

Discussion

Discuss the following questions as a class.

1. Do people ever give clothes as gifts in your country? If so, what kind of clothes? On what occasion(s)?
2. Do you enjoy receiving clothes as a gift? Why or why not?
3. Have you ever made any clothes? If so, what did you make?
4. What is the best gift you have ever received? Why was it special?

READING THE POEM

An *ode*, from a Greek word meaning "to sing," is a long poem that praises a person or thing. As you read "Ode to My Socks," think of it as a song the poet is singing in praise of a special pair of socks. Why does the poet praise his socks? Is his ode serious or funny?

Ode to My Socks

by Pablo Neruda
(translated by Robert Bly)

Maru Mori brought me
a pair
of socks
which she knitted herself
5   with her sheepherder's[1] hands,
two socks as soft
as rabbits.
I slipped my feet
into them
10   as though into
two
cases
knitted
with threads[2] of
15   twilight[3]
and goatskin.
Violent socks,
my feet were
two fish made
20   of wool,
two long sharks
sea-blue, shot

---

[1]**sheepherder** a shepherd, someone who takes care of sheep
[2]**threads** long, thin strings of wool, cotton, etc. used for knitting or sewing

[3]**twilight** the light in the sky between sunset and night

through
by one golden thread,
25 two immense[4] blackbirds,
two cannons:[5]
my feet
were honored
in this way
30 by
these
heavenly
socks.
They were
35 so handsome
for the first time
my feet seemed to me
unacceptable
like two decrepit[6]
40 firemen, firemen
unworthy
of that woven
fire,
of those glowing
45 socks.
Nevertheless
I resisted[7]
the sharp temptation[8]
to save them somewhere
50 as schoolboys
keep
fireflies,
as learned[9] men
collect
55 sacred texts,[10]
I resisted
the mad[11] impulse[12]

---

[4]**immense** very large
[5]**cannons** large guns, often on wheels
[6]**decrepit** old and in bad condition
[7]**resisted** opposed, fought
[8]**temptation** a strong desire to do something bad, silly, etc.

[9]**learned** scholarly, very educated
[10]**sacred text** a religious or special book
[11]**mad** crazy
[12]**impulse** a sudden desire to do something

to put them
into a golden
60 cage
and each day give them
birdseed
and pieces of pink melon.
Like explorers
65 in the jungle who hand
over[13] the very rare
green deer
to the spit[14]
and eat it
70 with remorse,[15]
I stretch out
my feet
and pull on
the magnificent
75 socks
and then my shoes.

The moral
of my ode is this:
beauty is twice
80 beauty
and what is good is doubly
good
when it is a matter[16] of two socks
made of wool
85 in winter.

[13]**hand over** give (something) to someone else
[14]**spit** a long, thin stick used for cooking meat over a
fire

[15]**remorse** regret, feeling sorry for doing something
bad or wrong
[16]**matter** an important subject or topic

THINKING ABOUT THE POEM

Comprehension

A. Discuss the following questions as a class.

1. Who gave the poet the socks?
2. Did she buy or make the socks?
3. What do you think her relationship to the poet is? Why?
4. How did the poet feel when he put on the socks? How do you know?
5. What season is it in the poem? How did this contribute to the poet's feelings?

B. Complete the following word map. Write adjectives the poet uses to describe his socks in the circles.

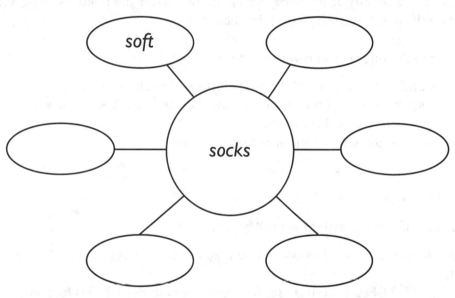

Focus on Reading: A Moral

Some stories, such as fables and folktales, end with a *moral*—a practical lesson about life. For example, in Aesop's fable *The Tortoise and the Hare*, the hare challenges the tortoise to a race. The hare is so sure he will win that he stops to sleep during the race. The tortoise, who keeps going at a slow and steady pace, passes the hare and wins the race. The moral of the story is "Slow and steady wins the race."

1. The poem ends with a moral. What lesson is the poet trying to teach? Restate the moral in your own words. Compare answers in small groups.
2. Do you know any fables or folktales that end with a moral? If so, tell the story to the class.

Focus on Literature: An Ode

> The word *ode* comes from the Greek word *aeidein*, which means "to sing." An ode is a kind of song—a poem full of emotion, which is usually written in praise of a person or thing. Many ancient odes were written to praise athletes, and they were sung and danced by a Greek chorus. Traditional odes were serious, but modern odes can be serious or funny, depending on the subject the poet is writing about and on the poet's attitude toward the subject.

Discuss the following questions with a partner.

1. In this ode, what are some of the poet's feelings about his new socks?
2. Think about the title of the poem and how the poet describes his socks. What is his attitude toward his socks? Explain.
3. Do you think this ode is serious or funny? Explain.

Expansion

Discuss the following questions in small groups.

1. Find the simile in lines 1–8. What two things does the poet compare? How are they alike?
2. In lines 17–33, Pablo Neruda uses four metaphors to describe his feet when he puts on the socks. Find the metaphors and circle them. (If necessary, reread the definition of *metaphor* on page 16.) What four things does the poet compare his feet to?
3. What temptation did the poet resist? Why did he call it a temptation? Why did he resist it?

RESPONDING TO THE POEM

Write about one of the following topics.

1. **Ode to My . . . .** Using "Ode to My Socks" as a model, write an ode to a special article of clothing. Use the following steps and your own ideas.

   • Make a word map with adjectives describing a special article of clothing. Use the word map on page 71 as a model.

- Write metaphors and similes to describe the article of clothing.
- Start your poem by explaining how you got the article of clothing.
- Describe how you feel about the article of clothing. Use adjectives, metaphors, and similes.
- Is there any moral or practical lesson you want to teach your readers? If so, use it to end your ode.

2. **A Special Gift.** Write a paragraph about a special gift you have received. Describe the gift and explain who gave it to you. Explain why the gift was special to you.

3. **Famous Clothes.** Is your country famous for any special clothes—for example, leather items, wool sweaters, embroidered shirts? Write a paragraph describing the clothes. Use the following questions to help you.

- What is special about them?
- Where are the clothes made?
- Do you ever wear these clothes? If so, when?

Peer Response

Work with a partner. Exchange papers and read each other's writing. Discuss the following questions.

- What adjectives does the writer use to describe the gift or article of clothing?
- Does the writer use any similes or metaphors?
- Is there a moral? If so, what does it teach?
- Do you have any questions for the writer?
- What do you like best about the writing?

After you discuss your ideas, you may want to revise your writing.

About the Author

Chilean poet Pablo Neruda (1904–1973) is famous for his odes and other poetry about everyday subjects. He won the Nobel Prize for Literature in 1971. In addition to writing poetry, Pablo Neruda served as a diplomat in many countries, including Burma (now Myanmar), Ceylon (now Sri Lanka), Indonesia, Singapore, Argentina, Spain, France, and Mexico.

Getups

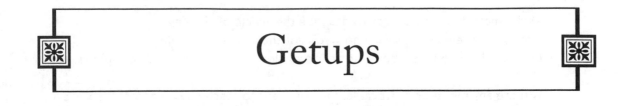

SETTING THE CONTEXT

Discussion

A. Discuss the following questions as a class.

1. Look at the people in the picture. Describe their clothes.
2. According to an English saying, "Clothes make the man." Do you think people's clothes influence how people see them? If so, how?
3. Do you form opinions about people based on their clothes? Explain.
4. Look at the people in the picture again. Do you think their clothes say anything about them? Explain.

B. Read the following statements. Check (✓) those that are true for you. Then discuss your answers in small groups.

I choose clothes . . .

_____ that feel comfortable.

_____ to identify with a particular group.

_____ that are fashionable.

_____ that make me look attractive.

_____ that are well made.

_____ to look different from other people.

_____ that are good value for the money.

_____ that express my creativity.

Vocabulary

The boldfaced words in the following sentences are from the essay on pages 76–78. Use the context to guess the meanings of the boldfaced words. Use a dictionary if necessary. Then match each boldfaced word with the correct definition that follows. Compare your answers in small groups.

_____ 1. High school students often want to **conform**; they want to act and dress like their friends.

_____ 2. Mrs. Smith has some **eccentric** habits, such as dressing her pets in matching clothes.

_____ 3. John and Mary wanted their romance to be secret, so they were very **discreet** about where they met.

_____ 4. My brother **concocted** a dessert by combining ice cream, fruit, chocolate sauce, and nuts.

_____ 5. When Bob failed a test, his sister made the **snide** remark that he studied too much television.

_____ 6. Painting a house really **enhances** its appearance.

_____ 7. Many companies now allow employees to wear casual clothing instead of their usual business **attire** on Fridays.

_____ 8. Children who are **neglected** by their parents often try hard to get attention at school.

_____ 9. Robert **desperately** wants to be a good student, so he studies very hard.

_____ 10. In hot weather, cotton is a more comfortable **fabric** than wool.

a. made something unusual by mixing different things together
b. ignored
c. clothes
d. very much
e. behave the same way as most people
f. strange or unusual
g. careful
h. material used to make clothes
i. improves, makes better
j. funny, but unkind

READING THE ESSAY

As you read the essay, think about the title. How does the author explain what *getups* means? Does she give a definition? Examples? Descriptions?

Getups

by Maya Angelou

1   I was a twenty-one-year-old single parent with my son in kindergarten. Two jobs allowed me an apartment, food, and child care[1] payment. Little money was left over for clothes, but I kept us nicely dressed in discoveries bought at the Salvation Army[2] and other second-hand[3] shops. Loving colors, I bought for myself beautiful reds and oranges, and greens and pinks, and teals and turquoise. I chose azure dresses and blouses and sweaters. And quite often I wore them in mixtures which brought surprise, to say the least, to the eyes of people who could not avoid noticing me. In fact, I concocted what southern black women used to call "getups."

[1]**child care** an arrangement in which someone takes care of children while the parents are working
[2]**Salvation Army** an organization that tries to help poor people

[3]**second-hand shop** a store that sells used items, such as clothes, at cheap prices

2   Because I was very keen[4] that my son not feel that he was neglected or different, I went frequently to his school. Sometimes between my jobs I would just go and stand outside the fenced play area. And he would, I am happy to say, always come and acknowledge me in the colorful regalia.[5] I always wore beads. Lots of beads. The cheaper they were, the more I got, and sometimes I wore head wraps.

3   When my son was six and I was twenty-two, he told me quite solemnly[6] that he had to talk to me. We both sat down at the kitchen table, and he asked with an old man's eyes and a young boy's voice, "Mother, do you have any sweaters that match?" I was puzzled at first. I said, "no," and then I understood he was talking about the pullover[7] and cardigan[8] sets which were popular with white women. And I said, "No, I don't," maybe a little too huffily.[9] And he said, "Oh I wish you did. So that you could wear them to school when you come to see me."

4   I was tickled,[10] but I am glad I didn't laugh because he continued, "Mother, could you please only come to school when they call you?" Then I realized that my attire, which delighted my heart and certainly activated my creativity, was an embarrassment to him.

5   When people are young, they desperately need to conform, and no one can embarrass a young person in public so much as an adult to whom he or she is related. Any outré[11] action or wearing of "getups" can make a young person burn[12] with self-consciousness.

6   I learned to be a little more discreet to avoid causing him displeasure. As he grew older and more confident, I gradually returned to what friends thought of as my eccentric way of dressing. I was happier when I chose and created my own fashion.

7   I have lived in this body all my life and know it much better than any fashion designer. I think I know what looks good on me, and I certainly know what feels good in me.

8   I appreciate the creativity which is employed in the design of fabric and the design of clothes, and when something does fit my body and personality, I rush to it, buy it quickly, and wear it frequently. But I must not lie to myself for fashion's sake. I am only willing to purchase the item which becomes[13] me and to wear that which enhances my image of myself to myself.

---

[4]**keen** very interested or eager
[5]**regalia** special or unusual clothes
[6]**solemnly** very seriously
[7]**pullover** a sweater without buttons
[8]**cardigan** a sweater with buttons at the front

[9]**huffily** angrily
[10]**tickled** pleased or amused
[11]**outré** something unusual and slightly shocking
[12]**burn** to feel embarrassed
[13]**become** to look good on someone

9   If I am comfortable inside my skin, I have the ability to make other people comfortable inside their skins although their feelings are not my primary reason for making my fashion choice. If I feel good inside my skin and clothes, I am thus free to allow my body its sway,[14] its natural grace, its natural gesture. Then I am so comfortable that whatever I wear looks good on me even to the external fashion arbiters.[15]

10   Dress is important to mention because many people are imprisoned by powerful dictates[16] on what is right and proper to wear. Those decisions made by others and sometimes at their convenience are not truly meant to make life better or finer or more graceful or more gracious. Many times they stem from greed, insensitivity, and the need for control.

11   I have been in company, not long to be sure, but in company where a purveyor[17] of taste[18] will look at a woman or man who enters a room and will say with a sneer, "That was last year's jacket." As hastily as possible, I leave that company, but not before I record the snide attitude which has nothing to do with the beauty or effectiveness of the garment,[19] but rather gives the speaker a moment's sense of superiority at, of course, someone else's expense.[20]

12   Seek the fashion which truly fits and befits[21] you. You will always be in fashion if you are true to yourself, and only if you are true to yourself. You might, of course, rightly wear that style which is emblazoned[22] on the pages of the fashion magazines of the day, or you might not.

13   The statement "Clothes make the man" should be looked at, reexamined, and in fact reevaluated. Clothes can make the man or woman look silly and foppish[23] and foolish. Try rather to be so much yourself that the clothes you choose increase your naturalness and grace.

---

[14]**sway** a swinging movement, from side to side
[15]**fashion arbiters** people who influence society's opinion about what is fashionable
[16]**dictates** rules or principles
[17]**purveyor** someone who supplies information or goods to people as a business
[18]**taste** the ability to judge good clothes, art, etc.

[19]**garment** an item of clothing
[20]**at someone else's expense** achieved by harming someone else
[21]**befit** to be appropriate or suitable for
[22]**emblazoned** shown in a clear, obvious way
[23]**foppish** too concerned about one's appearance

THINKING ABOUT THE ESSAY

Comprehension

Discuss the following questions as a class.

1. What can you infer about the author from this essay? Write five words to describe her.
2. Where did she buy clothes? Why?
3. How did the author feel about her clothes? Explain.
4. How did the author's son feel about her clothes? Explain.
5. Define *getups* in your own words. Give examples.
6. What is important to the author in buying clothes? Why?

Focus on Reading: Making Inferences

> As you learned in Unit 2, sometimes writers don't state information directly; they only imply or suggest it. In this case, we have to draw our own conclusions, or *make inferences* about what they mean. For example, if one character is listening to music and another character says, "The music is very loud," we can infer that he or she wants the first character to turn down the music.

Work with a partner. Read the following statements from "Getups." Make inferences about what each speaker really means. Write what you think each person means in your own words. (**Note:** More than one answer is possible.) Then compare answers as a class.

1. AUTHOR'S SON: "Mother, do you have any sweaters that match?" (paragraph 3)

    _____

    _____

2. AUTHOR'S SON: "Mother, could you please only come to school when they call you?" (paragraph 4)

    _____

    _____

3. PURVEYOR OF TASTE: "That was last year's jacket." (paragraph 11)

    _____

    _____

Focus on Literature: Thesis and Antithesis

When writing an essay, a writer usually has a *thesis*. This thesis presents the main argument or opinion about a particular subject. The writer sometimes follows the thesis with an *antithesis*, or counter-argument, to clarify or balance the thesis. For example, in paragraphs 6–9 of "Getups," Maya Angelou presents her thesis about fashion. In paragraphs 10–11, she presents an antithesis to clarify her thesis.

Work with a partner. Answer the following questions.

1. Reread paragraphs 6–9. Check (✓) the statement that best expresses the thesis.

   _____ a. People should wear clothes that have creative designs.

   _____ b. People should wear discreet clothing that doesn't embarrass others.

   _____ c. People should wear clothes that make them feel good.

2. Reread paragraphs 10–11. Check (✓) the statement that best expresses the antithesis.

   _____ a. People who know what's fashionable are superior to others.

   _____ b. People shouldn't let fashion experts tell them what to wear.

   _____ c. Fashion experts try to improve people's lives.

3. Reread paragraphs 12–13. The author concludes the essay by restating her thesis and antithesis. Underline the statement(s) that express(es) the thesis once. Underline the statement(s) that express(es) the antithesis twice.

Expansion

Discuss the following questions in small groups.

1. What kind of clothes do you like to wear?
2. Why do you like to wear them?
3. Sometimes people wear clothes in an unusual, noticeable way to show their feelings, attitudes, and opinions. We can say that they are trying to make a *fashion statement*. For example, a pop star's clothes might say, "I'm glamorous." Do you think your clothes make a fashion statement? Explain.

RESPONDING TO THE ESSAY

Write about one of the following topics.

1. **A Fashion Statement.** What is your opinion about fashion? Using "Getups" as a model, write an essay about it. Use the following questions to help you.

   - What kind of clothes do you like to wear? Why?
   - What factors are important to you in choosing your clothes? What factors are not important?
   - Do you think your clothes make a fashion statement? If so, what is it?
   - Do you have a personal story that illustrates your opinion about clothes? If so, use it in your essay.

2. **Sayings about Clothes.** Maya Angelou mentions the English saying "Clothes make the man." Do you know a saying about clothes in another language? If so, write a paragraph or essay about it. Use the following questions to help you.

   - What does the saying mean?
   - What does the saying show about some people's opinions?
   - Do you have a personal experience that illustrates this saying? If so, include it.
   - Do you agree with the saying? Why or why not?

3. **What Was I Thinking?** Have you ever bought clothes that didn't suit you and you later regretted buying? Write a paragraph or essay about the experience. Use the following questions to help you.

   - What did you buy?
   - Why did you buy the clothes?
   - How did you feel when you wore the clothes?
   - Did other people react to the clothes? If so, how?
   - Did you ever wear the clothes again?
   - What did you learn from the experience?

Peer Response

Work with a partner. Exchange papers and read each other's writing. Discuss the following questions.

- Does the writer have a thesis? If so, what is it?
- Does the writer have an antithesis? If so, what is it?
- What did you learn about the writer?
- Do you have any questions for the writer?
- What do you like best about the writing?

After you discuss your ideas, you may want to revise your writing.

About the Author

Born in Stamps, Arkansas, Maya Angelou is a writer of poetry, essays, autobiographies, and plays. She is also an educator, historian, actress, producer, director, and civil-rights activist. Her many books include *I Know Why the Caged Bird Sings* and *Even the Stars Look Lonesome*. "Getups" is from her collection *Wouldn't Take Nothing for My Journey Now*.

Girl with the Green Skirt

SETTING THE CONTEXT

Discussion

Discuss the following questions as a class.

1. Describe the picture. What is the woman doing? What are the men doing?
2. How do you think the woman feels? Why?
3. Have you ever worn a special or unusual item of clothing? If so, what did you wear? Did other people notice you? If so, how did you feel?
4. Do you usually notice other people's reactions to your clothes? Why or why not?

READING THE POEM

As you read the poem, try to imagine what the woman looks like and how she is acting.

Girl with the Green Skirt

by Dana Naone

She walks down the road,
her green skirt floating around her knees.

The men she passes peel off[1] their shirts
and jump into her wide green hem.[2]

5   She keeps walking, her skirt
clear as the surface of a pond.[3]

Now they hold their arms out from their sides
like the branches of a tree, but no one is fooled
when the birds fly past them and nest[4]

10   in the green forest of her skirt.

Unaware of the hot wind swirling[5] around
the cool skirt keeps going.
The men following behind are thirsty
for the water of crushed[6] leaves.

15   Falling into the deep grass
they want to live with green forever.

[1]**peel off** take off
[2]**hem** edge of a piece of cloth, such as the bottom of a skirt
[3]**pond** small body of water

[4]**nest** sit close together
[5]**swirling** turning around in circles
[6]**crushed** broken in very small pieces

THINKING ABOUT THE POEM

Comprehension

Discuss the following questions as a class.

1. What does the woman do at the beginning of the poem?
2. What do the men she passes do first?
3. Do you think she notices the men? Why or why not?
4. What do the men do next? Does she notice them now?
5. What do the men finally do? Why do you think they do this?

Focus on Literature: Figures of Speech

Figures of speech are expressions that create strong images in the reader's mind. Writers, especially poets, often use figures of speech to make unusual comparisons between two things. Four common figures of speech are *similes*, *metaphors*, *metonyms*, and *oxymorons*.

A *simile* makes a comparison using the words *like* or *as*. For example:

> Her hair was **as** dark **as** night.

A *metaphor* makes a comparison without using *like* or *as*. For example:

> He cried a **river** of **tears**.

A *metonym* replaces the name of one thing with the name of something related to it. For example:

> In 1775, the American colonies belonged to **the crown**.

In this example, *the crown* replaces *the king* (in this case, King George III of England).

An *oxymoron* combines two contrasting words or ideas. For example:

> The **silence** in the classroom was **deafening**.

> The more **things change**, the more **they stay the same**.

A. Work with a partner. Reread the poem and answer the following questions.

1. Underline the simile in lines 5–6. What two things are compared? How are they alike?
2. Underline the simile in lines 7–8. What two things are compared? How are they alike?
3. Underline the metaphor in line 10. What two things are compared? How are they alike?
4. Underline the metonym in line 12. What word does *skirt* replace?
5. Underline the oxymoron in lines 13–14. What contrasting things are combined?
6. Underline the metonym in line 16. What word does *green* replace?

B. Work in small groups. Look at the figures of speech you underlined. Why do you think Dana Naone chose them? How do they affect you as a reader?

Focus on Reading: Making Inferences

As you've learned, sometimes writers don't state information directly; they only suggest it. We have to draw our own conclusions, or *make inferences,* about what they mean. In "Girl with the Green Skirt," Dana Naone doesn't directly tell us much about the woman. However, she suggests things about her by using images and figures of speech. As readers, we have to make inferences based on these images.

Work with a partner. Discuss the following questions. Use details from the poem to support your answers. Then compare answers as a class.

1. How old do you think the woman is? Why?
2. Where do you think this scene takes place? Why?
3. What do you think the weather is like? Why?
4. What do you think the woman looks like? What do you think her personality is like?
5. How old do you think the men are?

Expansion

1. What does the color green make you think of? Why?
2. Do you think any of the men in the poem will attract the woman? Why or why not?
3. What do you think the woman will do after she walks away?
4. What do you think the men will do after the woman walks away?

RESPONDING TO THE POEM

Write about one of the following topics.

1. **Looking Good.** Using "Girl with the Green Skirt" as a model, write a poem about a time when you think you looked good. Use the following questions to help you.

   • Where were you?
   • What were you doing?
   • What were you wearing?
   • How did other people react to your clothes?
   • How did their reactions make you feel?

   If possible, use images and figures of speech in your poem. You can write about yourself using the first-person *I* or the third-person *he* or *she.*

2. **The Man/Woman with the ...** Find a newspaper or magazine picture of someone wearing clothes that you find interesting, unusual, or attractive. Write a poem, paragraph, or essay about the person and the clothes. Use the following questions to help you.

   • What is the person wearing? What color is it?
   • What is the person doing? (Use your imagination.)
   • How does the person feel about the clothing? Make inferences from the picture.
   • How are other people reacting to the person and the clothes?

   If possible, use images and figures of speech in your poem, paragraph, or essay.

3. **A Letter.** Imagine that you are one of the men in the poem. Write a letter to the woman in the poem. Although she didn't notice you, you really want to talk to her. Tell her how you felt when you saw her walking by.

Peer Response

Work with a partner. Exchange papers and read each other's writing. Discuss the following questions.

   • What descriptive images does the writer use?
   • Does the writer use any figures of speech? If so, what are they?
   • Can you make any inferences based on the writer's images or figures of speech? If so, what are they?
   • Do you have any questions for the writer?
   • What do you like best about the writing?

After you discuss your ideas, you may want to revise your writing.

About the Author

Dana Naone was born on the island of Oahu, and she has lived in Hawaii all her life. She is of Hawaiian, English, Chinese, and Portuguese descent. She is a former editor of *Hawaii Review*, which publishes the works of young Hawaiian writers, as well as writers from other places. She has also taught in the Poets in the Schools Program. Her poem "Girl with the Green Skirt" is from the anthology *Carriers of the Dream Wheel: Contemporary Native American Poetry*.

The Red Coat

SETTING THE CONTEXT

Discussion

Discuss the following questions as a class.

1. Was any article of clothing special to you when you were a child? If so, describe the article of clothing and explain why it was special.
2. Have you ever admired an article of clothing worn by another person? Explain.
3. Do you like going to parties? If so, what do you usually wear?

READING THE PLAY

As you read the play, think about the title. What is special about the red coat? Who finds the coat special? Why?

The Red Coat

by John Patrick Shanley

Characters

JOHN, seventeen-year-old boy
MARY, sixteen-year-old girl

Setting

A side street, nighttime

Nighttime on a side street. A street light shines[1] down on some steps through a green tree. Moonlight mixes in the shadows. A seventeen-year-old boy sits on the steps in a white shirt with a loosened skinny tie, in black dress pants, and black shoes. He is staring off.[2] His eyes are shining. A sixteen-year-old girl enters, in neighborhood party clothes: short skirt, blouse, penny loafers.

    *   *   *   *   *

JOHN: Hi, Mary.

MARY: Oh! I didn't see you there. You're hiding.

JOHN: Not from you, Mary.

MARY: Who from?

5 JOHN: Oh, nobody. I was up at Susan's party.

MARY: That's where I'm going.

JOHN: Oh.

MARY: Why did you leave?

JOHN: No reason.

10 MARY: You just gonna sit there?

JOHN: For a while.

MARY: Well, I'm going in.

JOHN: Oh, Okay . . . Oh! I'm not going in . . . I mean came out because . . . Oh, go in!

---

[1] **shine** to produce light, to appear bright

[2] **staring off** looking steadily into the distance for a long time

15 MARY: What's wrong with you, John?

JOHN: I left the party because you weren't there. That's why I left the party.

MARY: Why'd ya leave the party 'cause I wasn't there?

JOHN: I dunno.

20 MARY: I'm going in.

JOHN: I left the party 'cause I felt everything I wanted was outside the party . . . out here. There's a breeze out here, and the moon . . . look at the way the moon is . . . and I knew you were outside somewhere, too! So I came out and sat on the steps here and I
25   thought that maybe you'd come and I would be here . . . outside the party, on the steps, in the moonlight . . . and those other people . . . the ones at the party . . . wouldn't be here . . . but the night would be here . . . and you and me would be talking on the steps in the night in the moonlight and I could tell you . . .

30 MARY: Tell me what?

JOHN: How I feel!

MARY: How you feel about what?

JOHN: I don't know. I was looking out the window at the party . . . and I drank some wine . . . and I was looking out the window at the
35   moon and I thought of you . . . and I could feel my heart . . . breaking.

MARY: Joh . . .

JOHN: I felt that wine and the moon and your face all pushing in my heart and I left the party and I came out here.

40 MARY: Your eyes are all shiny.

JOHN: I know. And I came out here looking for the moon and I saw that street light shining down through the leaves of that tree.

MARY: Hey yeah! It does look pretty.

JOHN: It's beautiful. I didn't know a street lamp could be beautiful. I've
45   always thought of them as being cold and blue, you know? But

this one's yellow . . . and it comes down through the leaves and the leaves are so green! Mary, I love you!

MARY: Oh!

JOHN: I shouldn't've said it. I shouldn't've said it.

50   MARY: No, no. That's all right.

JOHN: My heart's breaking. You must think I'm so stupid . . . but I can feel it breaking. I wish I could stop talking. I can't. I can't.

MARY: I never heard you talking like this before.

JOHN: That's 'cause this is outside the party and it's night and there's a
55   moon up there . . . and a street light that's more beautiful than the sun! My God, the sidewalk's beautiful. Those bits³ of shiny stuff⁴ in the concrete⁵ . . . look how they're sparkling⁶ up the light!

MARY: You're crying! You're crying over the sidewalk!

60   JOHN: I love you, Mary!

MARY: That's all right. But don't cry over the sidewalk. You're usually so quiet.

JOHN: Okay. Okay. *(A pause. Then John grabs Mary and kisses her.)*

MARY: Oh . . . you used your tongue. *(He kisses her again.)* You . . . should
65   we go into the party?

JOHN: No.

MARY: I got all dressed . . . I tasted the wine on your . . . mouth. You were waiting for me out here? I wasn't even going to come. I don't like Susan so much. I was going to stay home and watch a
70   movie. What would you have done?

JOHN: I don't know. *(Kisses her again. She kisses him back.)*

MARY: You go to St. Nicholas of Tolentine,⁷ don't you?

JOHN: Yeah.

---

³**bits** small pieces
⁴**stuff** *(informal)* substance or material
⁵**concrete** material used for building made of sand, small stones, cement, and water

⁶**sparkling** shining in small flashes, like a diamond
⁷**St. Nicholas of Tolentine** a Catholic high school

MARY: I see you on the platform[8] on a Hundred and Forty-ninth
75   Street sometimes.

JOHN: I see you, too! Sometimes I just let the trains go by until the last
        minute, hoping to see you.

MARY: Really?

JOHN: Yeah.

80 MARY: I take a look around for you but I always get on my train. What
          would you have done if I hadn't come?

JOHN: I don't know. Walked around. I walk around a lot.

MARY: Walk around where?

JOHN: I walk around your block[9] a lot. Sometimes I run into[10] you.

85 MARY: You mean that was *planned?* Wow! I always thought you were
          coming from somewhere.

JOHN: I love you, Mary. I can't believe I'm saying it . . . to you . . . out
        loud. I love you.

MARY: Kiss me again. *(They kiss.)*

90 JOHN: I've loved you for a long time.

MARY: How long?

JOHN: Months. Remember that big snowball fight?[11]

MARY: In the park?

JOHN: Yeah. That's when it was. That's when I fell in love with you. You
95   were wearing a red coat.

MARY: Oh, that coat! I've had that for ages and ages. I've had it since the
          sixth grade.

JOHN: Really?

[8]**platform** the raised part of the subway where
people get on and off the train
[9]**block** a square or rectangular area of houses or
buildings formed by four streets

[10]**run into** *(informal)* to meet someone by chance
[11]**snowball fight** a form of play in which children
make balls of snow and throw them at each other

MARY: I have really special feelings for that coat. I feel like it's part of
100   me . . . like it stands for something . . . my childhood . . .
       something like that.

JOHN: You look nice in that coat. I think I sensed something about
       it . . . the coat . . . it's special to me, too. It's so good to be able to
       talk to you like this.

105 MARY: Yeah, this is nice. That's funny how you felt that about my coat.
       The red one. No one knows how I feel about that coat.

JOHN: I think I do, Mary.

MARY: Do you? If you understood about my red coat . . . that red coat is
       like all the good things about when I was a kid . . . it's like I still
110   have all the good kid things when I'm in that red coat . . . it's like
       being grown up and having your childhood, too. You know what
       it's like? It's like being in one of those movies where you're safe,
       even when you're in an adventure. Do you know what I mean?
       Sometimes, in a movie the hero's[12] doin' all this stuff that's
115   dangerous,[13] but you know, becausa the kind of movie it is, that
       he's not gonna get hurt. Bein' in that red coat is like that . . . like
       bein' safe in an adventure.

JOHN: And that's the way you were in that snowball fight! It was like
       you knew that nothing could go wrong!

120 MARY: That's right! That's right! That's the way it feels! Oh, you do
       understand! It seems silly but I've always wanted someone to
       understand some things and that was one of them . . . the red
       coat.

JOHN: I do understand! I do!

125 MARY: I don't know. I don't know. I don't know about tomorrow, but . . .
       right this minute I . . . love you!

JOHN: Oh, Mary!

MARY: Oh, kiss me, John. Please!

JOHN: You're crying!

---

[12]**hero** the most important character in a book, play, or movie

[13]**stuff that's dangerous** dangerous activities

130 MARY: I didn't know. I didn't know two people could understand some things . . . share some things. *(They kiss.)*

JOHN: It must be terrible not to.

MARY: What?

JOHN: Be able to share things.

135 MARY: It is! It is! But don't you remember? Only a few minutes ago we were alone. I feel like I could tell you anything. Isn't that crazy?

JOHN: Do you want to go for a walk?

MARY: No, no. Let's stay right here. Between the street light and the moon. Under the tree. Tell me that you love me.

140 JOHN: I love you.

MARY: I love you, too. You're good-looking, did you know that? Does your mother tell you that?

JOHN: Yeah, she does.

MARY: Your eyes are shining.

145 JOHN: I know. I can feel them shining.

(The lights go down slowly.)

THINKING ABOUT THE PLAY

Comprehension

Discuss the following questions as a class.

1. Why did John leave the party?
2. What did John suddenly tell Mary?
3. When did John fall in love with Mary?
4. What specific thing did he remember about that experience?
5. Why was this thing special to John?
6. Why was it special to Mary?
7. What has Mary always wanted someone to understand? Why?

Focus on Reading: Reduced Forms

In natural conversation, native English speakers often do not pronounce every word clearly. They may run two or more words together so they sound like one word. These pronunciation changes are called *reduced forms*. Writers often use reduced forms in plays and stories so that the characters' speech sounds natural.

Read the following sentences from the play. The boldfaced words are reduced forms. Work with a partner. Rewrite the sentences using complete, grammatically correct forms.

1. You just **gonna** sit there? (line 10)

   Are you just going to sit there?

2. **Why'd ya** leave the party **'cause** I wasn't there? (line 18)

   _____

   _____

3. I **dunno**. (line 19)

   _____

4. I **shouldn't've** said it. (line 49)

   _____

5. Sometimes, in a movie the hero's **doin'** all this stuff that's dangerous, but you know, **becausa** the kind of movie it is, that he's not **gonna** get hurt. (lines 114–116)

   _____

   _____

   _____

6. **Bein'** in the red coat is like that . . . like **bein'** safe in an adventure. (lines 116–117)

   _____

   _____

Focus on Literature: Backstory

How do actors prepare to play different characters in the theater, on TV, or in the movies? They often use a technique called *backstory*. Backstory is a kind of short biography or personal history that actors create for a character. This biography helps actors to know and understand the characters. Then, when they play the characters, their acting is more real, and the audience believes the actors really are the characters. For example, while Susan never appears in "The Red Coat," an actor might create the following backstory for her.

> *Susan is seventeen years old. She lives with her parents in an apartment in New York City. She is self-confident, has many friends, and likes to give parties. Susan goes to the same school as Mary. Susan met John through Mary. Susan isn't good friends with John or Mary, but she invites them to her party. Susan's parents don't know that she is having this party; they went away for the weekend. It is illegal for teenagers to drink alcohol, but Susan has wine at her party because she likes to break rules. She also likes to act like she is older than she is.*

Work with a partner. Write backstory for John or Mary. Use the following questions to help you.

- Who is John/Mary?
- What does he/she look like?
- What is his/her personality like?

Share your backstory with the class.

Expansion

Discuss the following questions in small groups.

1. If John hadn't run into Mary outside the party, do you think he ever would have told her he loved her? Explain.
2. John and Mary say that they sometimes look for each other in the subway. Have you ever looked for someone you didn't know well but wanted to see? If so, what happened?
3. Sometimes people's lives change through a twist of fate, or an unexpected event. For example, John's chance meeting with Mary outside Susan's party brings an unexpected result. Has a twist of fate ever caused a change in your life? If so, what happened?

RESPONDING TO THE PLAY

Write about one of the following topics.

1. **Special Clothes.** Write a poem, paragraph, or essay about an article of clothing that was special to you when you were growing up. Use the following questions to help you.

    - How did it look?
    - How did you feel when you wore it?
    - How was it special?
    - Did other people think it was special? If so, who?
    - What happened to it?

2. **A Twist of Fate.** Write a poem, paragraph, or essay about a twist of fate—an unexpected event—that caused a change in your life. Use the following questions to help you.

    - What was the twist of fate?
    - What change did it cause?
    - Did it change your life? If so, how?

3. **Scene from a Play.** Write a scene (part of a play) about special clothes, a twist of fate, or another topic related to "The Red Coat." Be sure to:

    - Begin with a paragraph that explains the setting. (See the top of page 89.)
    - Write the characters' names in capital letters before each line.
    - Give the actors stage directions. For example, this is a stage direction from line 63 of "The Red Coat": *(A pause. Then John grabs Mary and kisses her.)*

If appropriate, use reduced forms to make the characters' speech natural.

Peer Response

Work with a partner. Exchange papers and read each other's writing. Discuss the following questions.

- What characters does the writer introduce?
- Does the writer use any reduced forms?
- What details does the writer use? What do they help you understand?
- Do you have any questions for the writer?
- What do you like best about the writing?

After you discuss your ideas, you may want to revise your writing.

About the Author

Playwright, screenwriter, and director John Patrick Shanley is from New York City. His full-length plays include *The Big Funk, Beggars in the House of Plenty, Savage in Limbo, The Dreamer Examines His Pillow,* and *Danny and the Deep Blue Sea*. He has also written a variety of one-act plays, including *Missing/Kissing*. His screenplay *Five Corners* won a Special Jury Prize at the Barcelona Film Festival, and his screenplay *Moonstruck* won an Academy Award for Best Original Screenplay. "The Red Coat" is from a collection of six short plays called *Welcome to the Moon*.

ON FURTHER REFLECTION

Making Connections

Discuss the following questions.

1. Why do you think Pablo Neruda, Maya Angelou, the Girl with the Green Skirt, and Mary (in the red coat) chose their clothes? Complete the chart with the following reasons. (**Note:** You may use some reasons for more than one person.) Then compare and discuss your answers in small groups.

to feel comfortable	to identify with a particular group
to feel special	to look attractive
because they are well made	to look different from other people
because they are a good value	to express creativity

Pablo Neruda	Maya Angelou	Girl with the Green Skirt	Mary

2. How do you think the people listed below would describe the following characters in their special clothing? Write an adjective (for example, *glamorous*, *mysterious*). Then compare your answers in small groups. (**Note:** There are no right answers, so you can use your imagination.)

a. CHARACTER: Pablo Neruda in his handmade socks

Pablo Neruda's description: _____

Maru Mori's description: _____

b. CHARACTER: Maya Angelou in her getups

Maya Angelou's description: _____

her son's description: _____

c. CHARACTER: Girl with the Green Skirt

the girl's description: _____

the men's description: _____

d. CHARACTER: Mary in her red coat

Mary's description: _____

John's description: _____

3. Which character in this unit do you think was the most concerned about his or her clothes? The least concerned? Which character's attitude toward clothes is most similar to yours? Explain.

Connecting to the Community

Choose one of the following projects.

1. Does your community have an organization (for example, Goodwill or the Salvation Army) that gives or sells secondhand clothes to people who need clothing? If so, consider collecting secondhand clothing as a class and giving them to the organization.
2. Go to a mall or other place in your city or town where you can observe many people. What are people wearing? What fashion trends do you notice? Report your findings to the class.
3. Work in small groups. Make a questionnaire about clothes. For example, you could ask: What is your favorite article of clothing? How do you choose your clothes? Interview people in the community. Share their responses with the class.

Growing Up

*F*or most people, growing up is a very special time: Life is new, possibilities are endless, and every day is an adventure where fantasy and reality often mix. Growing up is also a time for learning, for taking on new responsibilities, for preparing to be "grown up."

The writers in this unit consider various aspects of growing up. First, poet Diane Kahanu recalls some childhood experiences on an island in Hawaii. Sociolinguist and writer Deborah Tannen discusses how the different ways boys and girls play affects the way they communicate as young adults. Judith Ortiz Cofer tells a story about how her grandmother taught her a new way of understanding the number zero. Finally, poet Richard Hugo describes the "magics" of a special stone that brings back memories from his childhood.

People grow up, but they don't have to stop growing. For the writers in this unit, an important part of growing up is staying in touch with the ability to see the world through a child's eyes and to see life as continual discovery.

When I Was Young on an Island

SETTING THE CONTEXT

Discussion

Discuss the following questions as a class.

1. Who did you play with when you were a child?
2. What kinds of games did you play? Describe them.
3. Was there a leader among your friends? If so, what was this person like? How did he or she influence your activities?
4. Did anyone or anything ever get hurt in any of your games? If so, describe the experience.

READING THE POEM

As you read the poem, think about the poet's experiences. How were they similar to your experiences? How were they different? Also, think about the word *island* in the title. How did growing up on an island influence the poet's activities?

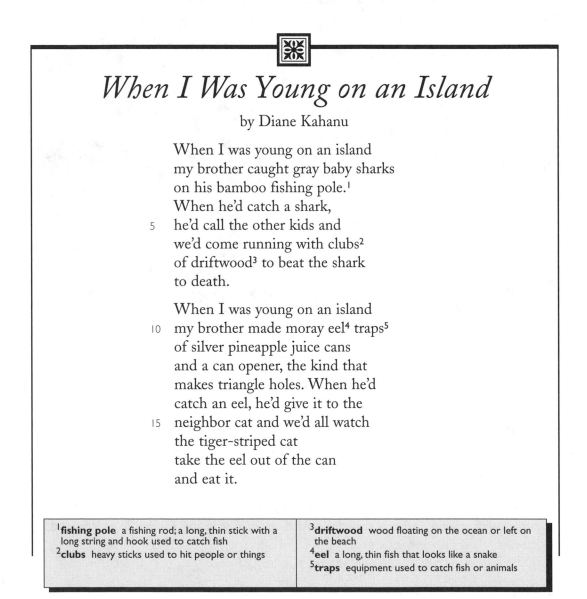

When I Was Young on an Island

by Diane Kahanu

When I was young on an island
my brother caught gray baby sharks
on his bamboo fishing pole.[1]
When he'd catch a shark,
5   he'd call the other kids and
we'd come running with clubs[2]
of driftwood[3] to beat the shark
to death.

When I was young on an island
10   my brother made moray eel[4] traps[5]
of silver pineapple juice cans
and a can opener, the kind that
makes triangle holes. When he'd
catch an eel, he'd give it to the
15   neighbor cat and we'd all watch
the tiger-striped cat
take the eel out of the can
and eat it.

[1] **fishing pole** a fishing rod; a long, thin stick with a long string and hook used to catch fish
[2] **clubs** heavy sticks used to hit people or things
[3] **driftwood** wood floating on the ocean or left on the beach
[4] **eel** a long, thin fish that looks like a snake
[5] **traps** equipment used to catch fish or animals

When we were young on Paiko Drive
20 in Kuli'ou'ou and we played war,
my brother invented the battle charge.[6]
He'd wait for a hard wind to pick
up the sand and just when the wind
was strongest, he'd yell, "Charge,"
25 and we'd run, head down, into a zillion[7]
tiny bullets of stinging[8] sand
hurled by the wind's hand.

When we were young on an island
my brother invented the jellyfish
30 test. He was an Apache Indian[9] that day.
Tortured,[10] he would not cry out.
We caught see-through jellyfish
in our hands and held them
while they stung us. Whoever
35 cried out first or dropped their
jellyfish lost. I remember sinking
to my knees with pain and finally
laying down in the cool shallow water.
Only my burning jellyfish hand
40 held out.

---

[6]**charge** an attack in which people move forward quickly

[7]**zillion** *(informal)* an extremely large number

[8]**stinging** causing sudden and very bad pain

[9]**Apache Indian** a Native American of the southwestern United States

[10]**tortured** hurt or injured on purpose

THINKING ABOUT THE POEM

Comprehension

Discuss the following questions as a class.

1. Notice how the poem is divided into four parts, or stanzas. What game or activity is described in each part?
2. Where does the poem take place? How does the location influence the games and activities?
3. Who is the main "character" in the poem?
4. How is the poet related to the main character?

Focus on Reading: Making Inferences

As you learned in Units 2 and 3, sometimes writers don't state information directly; they only imply or suggest it. In this case, the reader must *make inferences*—or form his or her own conclusions, based on the writers' examples and details. For example, in "When I Was Young on an Island," Diane Kahanu doesn't comment directly about the children's economic status. However, by looking at the children's games and activities, we might infer that they didn't have a lot of money to buy toys because they played with things like driftwood and a can opener.

Discuss the following questions in small groups.

1. What examples or details are given about the poet? What inferences can you make about her?
2. What examples or details are given about the poet's brother? What inferences can you make about him?
3. Can you make any inferences about the poet's relationship with her brother? If so, what are they?
4. What examples or details are given about life on an island? What inferences can you make about the children's lives?

Focus on Literature: Literal and Figurative Meanings

The term *literal* refers to the usual meaning of a word or phrase. For example, in the sentence *Sugar is sweet,* the word *sweet* has the usual or literal meaning (that is, tasting like sugar). In contrast, *figurative* refers to a special meaning of a word or phrase. Poets use figurative meaning to create strong images in the reader's mind. They create these images by using metaphors, similes, and personification. For example, the sentence *The wind sings sweetly* expresses figurative meaning by using personification. The sentence *She is as sweet as honey* expresses figurative meaning by using a simile.

The following statements are from the poem. Write *L* if the statement expresses a literal meaning. Write *F* if it expresses a figurative meaning. If you wrote *F*, underline the metaphor, simile, or personification that expresses the figurative meaning. Then compare answers in pairs.

_____ 1. We'd come running with clubs of driftwood to beat the shark to death.

_____ 2. My brother made moray eel traps of silver pineapple cans.

_____ 3. We'd run, head down, into a zillion tiny bullets of stinging sand hurled by the wind's hand.

_____ 4. He was an Apache Indian that day.

_____ 5. We caught see-through jellyfish in our hands and held them while they stung us.

Expansion

Discuss the following questions in small groups.

1. Do you think the poet passed the jellyfish test at the end of the poem? Explain.
2. If you were one of the children, would you take the jellyfish test? Explain.
3. Children often experience *peer pressure,* or the feeling that they have to do what their friends do in order to be accepted. Did you ever participate in something because of peer pressure? If so, describe it. Would you do the same thing now? Explain.
4. The children in the poem sometimes hurt animals when they played. When you were young, did you or any of your friends ever hurt an animal? If so, describe the experience. How did you feel about it then? How do you feel about it now?
5. As you learned in Unit 2, sometimes writers use personification to describe a thing or quality as if it were a person. Reread lines 22–27. What is the poet describing? What human qualities does she give it?

RESPONDING TO THE POEM

Write about one of the following topics.

1. **When I Was Young.** Using "When I Was Young on an Island" as a model, write a poem about your childhood. Use the following questions to help you.

   • Where did you grow up?
   • How did this place influence your childhood activities?
   • Who did you play with?
   • Where did you play?
   • What games did you play?

   If you like, you can divide your poem into stanzas and describe a different activity in each part. You can also use metaphors, similes, and personification to express figurative meaning.

2. **Peer Pressure.** Have you ever done something you didn't want to do because of peer pressure? If so, write a paragraph or essay about it. Use the following questions to help you.

   • What was the situation?
   • What people were involved?
   • What did they want you to do?
   • Do you regret having done it? Explain.
   • What did you learn from the experience?

3. **A Test.** Have you ever participated (or refused to participate) in a test that a friend invented? If so, write a paragraph or essay about it. Use the following questions to help you.

   • Who invented the test?
   • What was its purpose?
   • How did a person pass or fail the test?
   • Did you participate in the test? Why or why not?
   • What did you learn from the experience?

Peer Response

Work with a partner. Exchange papers and read each other's writing. Discuss the following questions.

   • Are there any words or phrases that express figurative meaning?
   • What did you learn about the writer?
   • Can you make any inferences about the writer's childhood? If so, what are they?
   • Do you have any questions for the writer?
   • What do you like best about the writing?

After you discuss your ideas, you may want to revise your writing.

About the Author

Diane Kahanu grew up in Hawaii. Her brother, Wayne, was her role model when she was growing up. "When I Was Young on an Island" appears in the anthology *Sister Stew: Fiction and Poetry by Women*.

Why Boys Don't Know What Girls Mean and Girls Think Boys are Mean

SETTING THE CONTEXT

Discussion

Discuss the following questions as a class.

1. Describe the boy in the picture. What is he doing?
2. Describe the girl in the picture. What is she doing?
3. What differences do you notice between the boy's and girl's activities?

Vocabulary

A. The words in Lists A and B are from the essay on pages 109–113. Work with a partner. Match the words with similar meanings. Use a dictionary if necessary.

List A	List B
_f_ 1. mean	a. results
____ 2. ruined	b. fun
____ 3. shield	c. unimportant
____ 4. kids	d. children
____ 5. buddies	e. protect
____ 6. consequences	f. hurtful
____ 7. amusing	g. friends
____ 8. insignificant	h. destroyed

B. Complete each sentence with the correct word from List A above. Then compare answers in small groups.

1. Those people are so _____ mean _____! They don't care about other people.

2. We had a great family vacation! Our _____ really enjoyed it.

3. The earthquake _____ the Smiths' house. Now they don't know where they're going to live.

4. Everything you say to children has _____. Think about how your words will affect them.

5. Parents try to _____ their children from danger.

6. When people look at the stars in the sky, they sometimes feel very _____.

7. Children don't always think the same game is _____. Some may like it, but others don't.

8. I went to the concert with my two best _____.

READING THE ESSAY

As you read the essay, think about the way you played when you were growing up. How did the way you played compare to the way the children in the essay played?

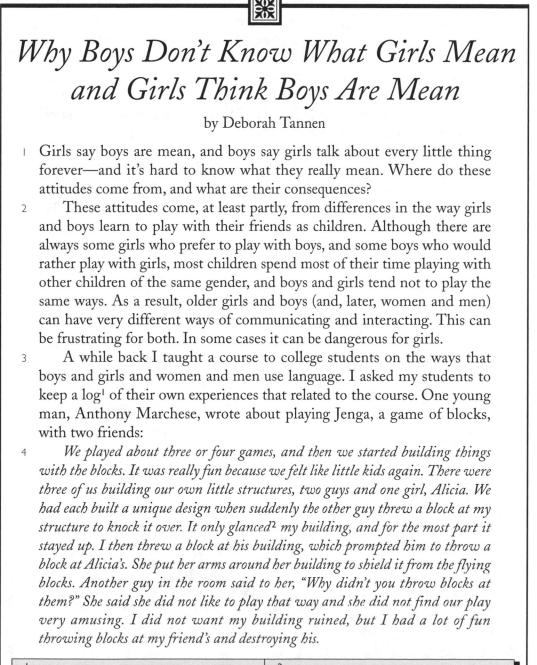

Why Boys Don't Know What Girls Mean and Girls Think Boys Are Mean

by Deborah Tannen

1   Girls say boys are mean, and boys say girls talk about every little thing forever—and it's hard to know what they really mean. Where do these attitudes come from, and what are their consequences?

2   These attitudes come, at least partly, from differences in the way girls and boys learn to play with their friends as children. Although there are always some girls who prefer to play with boys, and some boys who would rather play with girls, most children spend most of their time playing with other children of the same gender, and boys and girls tend not to play the same ways. As a result, older girls and boys (and, later, women and men) can have very different ways of communicating and interacting. This can be frustrating for both. In some cases it can be dangerous for girls.

3   A while back I taught a course to college students on the ways that boys and girls and women and men use language. I asked my students to keep a log[1] of their own experiences that related to the course. One young man, Anthony Marchese, wrote about playing Jenga, a game of blocks, with two friends:

4   *We played about three or four games, and then we started building things with the blocks. It was really fun because we felt like little kids again. There were three of us building our own little structures, two guys and one girl, Alicia. We had each built a unique design when suddenly the other guy threw a block at my structure to knock it over. It only glanced[2] my building, and for the most part it stayed up. I then threw a block at his building, which prompted him to throw a block at Alicia's. She put her arms around her building to shield it from the flying blocks. Another guy in the room said to her, "Why didn't you throw blocks at them?" She said she did not like to play that way and she did not find our play very amusing. I did not want my building ruined, but I had a lot of fun throwing blocks at my friend's and destroying his.*

---

[1] **log** a journal or notebook where you record information

[2] **glanced** touched quickly and lightly

5   Anthony realized he was playing the way he had played as a child. Part of the fun was building his own structure, but another part was destroying someone else's. Anthony and the other young man had the same idea of what was fun, but Alicia did not share that idea. Anthony guessed (correctly, I think) that when Alicia was a little girl, having fun with friends didn't include destroying each other's creations. This partly explains why when boys and girls try to play together, girls often end up thinking[3] boys are mean.

6   Now, what about boys' attitude that girls talk on and on about insignificant things, and that it's hard to know what they're getting at?[4]

7   Another one of my students, Aiyana Hoffman, took several classmates to her twelve-year-old cousin's birthday party. At one point there was a lot of commotion[5] at the party because one girl (I'll call her Mary) said something that hurt the feelings of another girl (I'll call her Sue). Sue felt so bad, she went into the bathroom, crying. Immediately the other girls were going in and out of the bathroom to check on Sue, to find out what was wrong and try to make her feel better. Sue's best friend (Kate) seemed to be in charge, speaking privately with all the other girls, reporting on Sue's feelings and even talking privately with Mary—the girl who had hurt Sue's feelings.

8   While the girls were caught up in[6] this drama, the boys were playing video games and, as my student Cortney Howard put it, "goofing off."[7] One boy (I'll call him Jason) was giving another boy (Joe) a hard time,[8] and two other boys joined in. Their conversation (which Cortney wrote down) went like this:

9   JASON: *So what's up with Karen? She's got you all whooped.[9]*

JOE: *No dude,[10] she's just some girl, nothin' special. I ain't whooped.*

JASON: *Yeah, you've been calling her. I saw you talking to her on the playground after school last week, too.*

JOE: *What are you talking about? I was just getting the math homework, that's all.*

JASON: *Horse crap![11] You like her!*

SAM: *Look, man, he's turning red! You're turning red! Ha-ha!*

JACK: *You wimp,[12] you're red all over that ugly face of yours!*

---

[3]**end up thinking** to conclude
[4]**getting at** suggesting
[5]**commotion** sudden noisy activity or arguing
[6]**caught up in** involved in
[7]**goofing off** (*informal*) wasting time or avoiding doing work
[8]**giving (someone) a hard time** criticizing or causing problems for someone

[9]**whooped** (*slang*) beaten or defeated
[10]**dude** (*slang*) man
[11]**Horse crap!** (*slang, impolite*) That's completely wrong!
[12]**wimp** (*slang*) someone who is afraid to do something

10   This conversation is different from the girls' in many ways. First of all, Jason insulted Joe openly, and the other boys joined in. When Mary said something to make Sue feel bad, she said it in private, and the other girls only found out later what it was. When they did, they tried to console[13] her.

11   And did you notice how the boys and girls reacted differently when their friends showed their feelings? When Joe turned red, it became another reason for the boys to put him down—to call him a wimp. Sue didn't hide her hurt. It gave her a kind of power when she cried in the bathroom. In a way she became the most important person at the party, and the bathroom became her headquarters! My students also noticed another difference between the boys and girls at the party. When they came upon Kate and Mary whispering in the laundry room, the girls immediately stopped talking, not wanting strangers to overhear[14] their secrets. But when the college students were listening in on Jason and his buddies, the boys "kind of acted up,"[15] as my student wrote, "as if they were playing in front of an important audience." This made me think about how many girls are reluctant to talk in front of others—for example, in class, where many boys actually compete to be called on, stretching their arms and even waving them or calling out.

12   The girls' way of negotiating their friendships and rivalries[16] was done in private conversations, but the boys' way emphasized showmanship,[17] which has to be done with an audience. Because the boys are used to playing out their rivalries publicly, they don't know what to make of[18] conversations like the girls at the party were having in the bathroom and laundry room. That explains, at least partly, why the boys think the girls go on and on about unimportant things. What's important to the girls— conversations about who said what to whom and how that made them feel—seems unimportant to the boys.

13   These two examples can help us understand what happens when boys and girls get together. At the birthday party the boys and girls tended to play separately, even though they were all at the same gathering. But when boys and girls get older, they spend more and more time together, either in groups or in pairs. Like the college students playing Jenga, they have different ideas of how to do things together and how to talk about what they want, and this makes things awkward or even dangerous, especially if the boys want to do something that the girls don't want to do.

---

[13]**console** to help someone who is sad feel better
[14]**overhear** to accidentally hear what others are saying without their knowledge
[15]**acted up** *(informal)* behaved badly

[16]**rivalry** continuous competition
[17]**showmanship** skill at entertaining people
[18]**what to make of** how to understand

14   When Anthony and his friend wanted to throw blocks and destroy each other's buildings, but Alicia didn't want to, she protected her building by shielding it with her arms. But it isn't always that simple. What if a boy wants to do something that has to do with sex and the girl doesn't want to? In a book called *The Difference*, Judy Mann tells about a study that really made me think. Two researchers named Marion Howard and Judith McCabe asked more than a thousand sexually active girls what they most wanted to have more information about. Rather than checking off contraception or the mechanics of sex, eighty-four percent checked this: "How to say no without hurting the other person's feelings."

15   If a boy wants a girl to do something she doesn't want to, this is what can happen: While she is trying to balance what she wants with her concern about his feelings and what he wants, he is concentrating only on what he wants and assumes that she will concentrate on what she wants. This imbalance is what can be dangerous. She probably doesn't realize that he is working by a different system, so she thinks that if she gives him a hint that she doesn't want to do something, he will pick up the hint and back off[19]—without his feelings getting hurt. But if he isn't used to communicating that way, he won't be listening for hints. The result can be that she does something she doesn't want to do, and he may never realize how much she didn't want to do it.

16   This might sound like another way of saying that boys are mean, that they're selfish and just go after what they want. But you don't have to look at it that way. If two people get together, and each one looks out for[20] himself or herself, it's a fair situation—the kind of situation most boys are used to, because that's the way they've been playing all their lives.

17   Think back to the birthday party. Remember how Sue's hurt feelings gave her so much power because all the girls were concerned with her feelings? That shows how girls learn, from early on, how to pay a lot of attention to others' feelings. When Joe showed his feelings by blushing,[21] the other boys used it against him, calling him a wimp. That shows how boys learn to hide or deny their feelings rather than pay extra attention to them.

18   Once girls understand the different ways that boys and girls interact, they should feel free to concentrate on what they want and don't want.

---

[19]**back off** to stop trying to make someone do or think something
[20]**look out for (someone)** to protect (someone)

[21]**blushing** turning red in the face, usually from embarrassment

19	And make it clear.
20	And insist on it.
21	It's fairer to themselves, and it's fairer to the boys, who often don't realize what girls are getting at when they try to say no without hurting boys' feelings.

THINKING ABOUT THE ESSAY

Comprehension

A. Complete each statement with *Girls, Boys,* or *Girls and Boys.* Then compare your answers in small groups.

1. _____ negotiate their friendships and rivalries privately.

2. _____ negotiate their friendships and rivalries publicly.

3. _____ have different ideas of how to do things together.

4. _____ like to destroy each other's creations.

5. _____ have different ideas of how to talk about what they want.

6. _____ concentrate on what they want.

7. _____ are concerned about hurting each others' feelings.

8. _____ learn to hide or deny their feelings.

9. _____ learn to pay attention to others' feelings.

10. _____ clearly say what they want and don't want.

B. Discuss the following questions as a class.

1. According to the author, what do girls say about boys? What do boys say about girls?
2. Where does she believe these attitudes come from?
3. What did Anthony Marchese observe from playing Jenga?
4. What did Aiyana Hoffman and Cortney Howard observe about the girls' and boys' ways of communicating at the birthday party?
5. Why does the author think these different ways of communicating can be dangerous for girls?
6. What does the author think girls should do?

Focus on Reading: Guessing Meaning from Context

As you learned in Unit 1, you can often guess the meaning of a word from the *context*—from the words and sentences around it. Sometimes the context gives:

- a definition of the word (the definition may follow a comma or dash)
- a synonym
- an example
- contrasting information about the word (the words *but* and *although* indicate contrasting information)

The following sentences are from the essay. Use the context to guess the meanings of the boldfaced words. Then compare your answers in small groups.

1. Anthony Marchese wrote about playing **Jenga**, a game of blocks, with two friends.

   Jenga: ___*a game of blocks*___

2. When Joe showed his feelings by blushing, the other boys called him a wimp. He soon learned to hide or **deny** feelings rather than call attention to them.

   deny: _____

3. At the birthday party the boys and girls tended to play separately, even though they were at the same **gathering**.

   gathering: _____

4. Jason **insulted** Joe openly, and the other boys joined in. When Mary said something to make Sue feel bad, she said it in private, and the other girls only found out later what it was.

   insulted: _____

5. Kate seemed to be **in charge**, speaking privately with all the other girls, reporting on Sue's feelings and even talking privately with Mary—the girl who had hurt Sue's feelings.

   in charge: _____

6. Anthony and the other young man had the same idea of what was fun, but Alicia did not **share** that idea.

   share: _____

7. Although there are always some girls who prefer to play with boys, and some boys who would rather play with girls, most children spend most of their time playing with other children of the same **gender**.

    gender:_____

Focus on Literature: Theme and Thesis

> The *theme* is the main idea or subject of an essay. For example, the theme might be love and friendship, childhood and adolescence, or money and happiness.
>
> The *thesis* is the writer's specific purpose in writing about the idea or subject. A thesis (1) presents the writer's main idea about the subject, (2) suggests what information will be included in the essay, and (3) often suggests how the essay will be organized. For example, one thesis on the theme of love and friendship might be "Friendship is more valuable than love because love is selfish." The reader can expect that the essay will include examples that support the writer's point of view. The examples will probably be organized in separate parts with examples of love versus friendship.

Discuss the following questions as a class.

1. What is the theme of Deborah Tannen's essay?
2. What is Deborah Tannen's thesis? Find it in the essay and underline it.
3. What information does the thesis suggest will be included?
4. How does the thesis suggest the essay will be organized?

Expansion

Discuss the following questions in small groups.

1. When you were growing up, how often did you play with boys? With girls? With both boys and girls?
2. Describe boys' and girls' playtime activities in your country. How are they similar to those described in the essay? How are they different?
3. Do you think these activities influence boys' and girls' attitudes when they grow up? If so, how?

Responding to the Essay

Write about one of the following topics.

1. **The Way We Played.** Write a paragraph or essay describing how children played when you were growing up.

   - How often did boys and girls play together?
   - What games did only boys play?
   - What games did only girls play?
   - What games did boys and girls play together?

   Then write a paragraph explaining how you think these activities influenced their ways of communicating when they became adults.

2. **Personal Observations.** Deborah Tannen's students kept a log with their observations about how boys and girls use language. Keep a log with your observations about how boys and girls (or men and women) communicate.

   - You can write a log entry describing the conversation, as Anthony did on page 109.
   - You can also write part of a conversation, as Cortney did on page 110.

   Then use your observations to write a paragraph or essay about how boys and girls (or men and women) communicate. What conclusions can you make about their attitudes?

3. **A Favorite Work.** Do you have a favorite movie, story, play, song, or poem that shows a difference between how men and women communicate? If so, write a paragraph or essay about it. Explain the theme of the work and its thesis. Then explain why you like it and how it shows how men and women are different.

Peer Response

Work with a partner. Exchange papers and read each other's writing. Discuss the following questions.

   - Is there a thesis? If so, what does it tell you about the writing?
   - Are there any new words? If so, can you guess their meanings from context?
   - Do you have any questions for the writer?
   - What do you like best about the writing?

After you discuss your ideas, you may want to revise your writing.

About the Author

Deborah Tannen is a sociolinguist and Professor of Linguistics at Georgetown University in Washington, D.C. Her book *You Just Don't Understand: Women and Men in Conversation* was on the *New York Times* bestseller list for almost four years, and it has been translated into twenty-four languages. In addition to her fourteen nonfiction books on language, she has published essays, short stories, plays, and poems.

Abuela Invents the Zero

SETTING THE CONTEXT

Discussion

Discuss the following questions as a class.

1. When you were a child, did you ever do any activities with your grandparents or other older relatives? If so, what did you do?
2. Did a grandparent or other older relative ever teach you something important? If so, what was it?
3. How do young people usually behave toward older people in your country? Give examples.
4. When you were a child, did any of your relatives ever do something that embarrassed you? Explain.

Vocabulary

A. The words in List A are from the story on pages 120–123. Work with a partner. Match the words in List A with the correct definitions from List B. Use a dictionary if necessary.

List A	List B
____ 1. support	a. act embarrassed by something
____ 2. lame	b. is very serious about something
____ 3. jerk	c. delivers or gives
____ 4. packed	d. becoming smaller
_a_ 5. cringe	e. provide enough money for someone to live
____ 6. compromise	f. stupid or unkind person
____ 7. retrieve	g. too silly or stupid to believe
____ 8. means business	h. completely full of people or things
____ 9. hands over	i. find and bring back
____ 10. shrinking	j. agreement

B. Complete each sentence with the correct word from List A above. Then compare answers in small groups.

1. Ted and Sarah had very different opinions, but finally they reached a _____.

2. The theater was _____; there was not one empty seat.

3. My clothes seem to be _____; maybe I should lose some weight.

4. Tom said, "The dog ate my homework." The teacher didn't accept his _____ excuse.

5. While I was driving my car, that _____ went through a red light and almost hit me.

6. John _____ his final paper to his professor tomorrow. Then he's finished with school.

7. I forgot my umbrella at the restaurant, but fortunately I was able to _____ it.

8. Our teacher will fail anyone who cheats on an exam; she _____.

9. It is often difficult for a single parent to _____ his or her family.

10. Whenever her aunt speaks too loudly, Natalie and her sister _____.

READING THE STORY

As you read the story, think about the title. What zero is Abuela talking about? Why does the author say that Abuela "invents" the zero? Also, notice the author's use of Spanish words in the story. Why do you think she uses them?

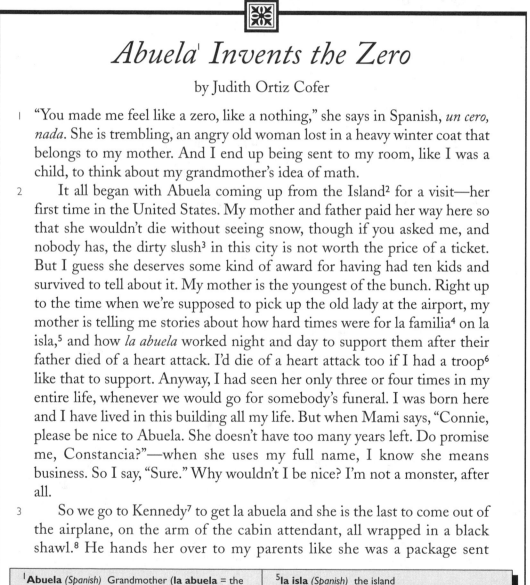

Abuela[1] *Invents the Zero*

by Judith Ortiz Cofer

1   "You made me feel like a zero, like a nothing," she says in Spanish, *un cero, nada.* She is trembling, an angry old woman lost in a heavy winter coat that belongs to my mother. And I end up being sent to my room, like I was a child, to think about my grandmother's idea of math.

2   It all began with Abuela coming up from the Island[2] for a visit—her first time in the United States. My mother and father paid her way here so that she wouldn't die without seeing snow, though if you asked me, and nobody has, the dirty slush[3] in this city is not worth the price of a ticket. But I guess she deserves some kind of award for having had ten kids and survived to tell about it. My mother is the youngest of the bunch. Right up to the time when we're supposed to pick up the old lady at the airport, my mother is telling me stories about how hard times were for la familia[4] on la isla,[5] and how *la abuela* worked night and day to support them after their father died of a heart attack. I'd die of a heart attack too if I had a troop[6] like that to support. Anyway, I had seen her only three or four times in my entire life, whenever we would go for somebody's funeral. I was born here and I have lived in this building all my life. But when Mami says, "Connie, please be nice to Abuela. She doesn't have too many years left. Do promise me, Constancia?"—when she uses my full name, I know she means business. So I say, "Sure." Why wouldn't I be nice? I'm not a monster, after all.

3   So we go to Kennedy[7] to get la abuela and she is the last to come out of the airplane, on the arm of the cabin attendant, all wrapped in a black shawl.[8] He hands her over to my parents like she was a package sent

[1] **Abuela** *(Spanish)* Grandmother (**la abuela** = the grandmother)
[2] **the Island** Puerto Rico *(familiar term used by Puerto Rican immigrants)*
[3] **slush** partly melted snow
[4] **la familia** *(Spanish)* the family
[5] **la isla** *(Spanish)* the island
[6] **troop** a group of people
[7] **Kennedy** John F. Kennedy Airport in New York City
[8] **shawl** a piece of cloth worn around the shoulders for warmth

airmail. It is January, two feet of snow on the ground, and she's wearing a shawl over a thin black dress. That's just the start.

4   Once home, she refuses to let my mother buy her a coat because it's a waste of money for the two weeks she'll be in *el Polo Norte*, as she calls New Jersey, the North Pole. So since she's only four feet eleven inches tall, she walks around in my mother's big black coat looking ridiculous. I try to walk far behind them in public so that no one will think we're together. I plan to stay very busy the whole time she's with us so that I won't be asked to take her anywhere, but my plan is ruined when my mother comes down with the flu and Abuela absolutely *has* to attend Sunday mass[9] or her soul will be eternally[10] damned.[11] She's more Catholic than the Pope.[12] My father decides that he should stay home with my mother and that I should escort la abuela to church. He tells me this on Saturday night as I'm getting ready to go out to the mall with my friends.

5   "No way," I say.

6   I go for the car keys on the kitchen table: he usually leaves them there for me on Friday and Saturday nights. He beats me to them.[13]

7   "No way," he says, pocketing them and grinning at me.

8   Needless to say, we come to a compromise very quickly. I do have a responsibility to Sandra and Anita, who don't drive yet. There is a Harley-Davidson fashion show at Brookline Square that we *cannot* miss.

9   "The mass in Spanish is at ten sharp[14] tomorrow morning, entiendes?"[15] My father is dangling the car keys in front of my nose and pulling them back when I try to reach for them. He's really enjoying himself.

10   "I understand. Ten o'clock. I'm out of here." I pry his fingers off the key ring. He knows that I'm late, so he makes it just a little difficult. Then he laughs. I run out of our apartment before he changes his mind. I have no idea what I'm getting myself into.

11   Sunday morning I have to walk two blocks on dirty snow to retrieve the car. I warm it up for Abuela as instructed by my parents, and drive it to the front of our building. My father walks her by the hand in baby steps on the slippery snow. The sight of her little head sticking out of that huge coat makes me want to run back into my room and get under the covers. I just hope that nobody I know sees us together. I'm dreaming, of course. The mass is packed with people from our block. It's a holy day of obligation and everyone I ever met is there.

---

[9]**mass** a Catholic religious ceremony
[10]**eternally** forever
[11]**damned** sent to hell
[12]**the Pope** the leader of the Roman Catholic church

[13]**beats me to them** does something before I can
[14]**sharp** exactly
[15]**entiendes?** *(Spanish)* Do you understand?

12   I have to help her climb the steps, and she stops to take a deep breath after each one, then I lead her down the aisle so that everybody can see me with my bizarre grandmother. If I were a good Catholic, I'm sure I'd get some purgatory[16] time taken off for my sacrifice. She is walking as slow as Captain Cousteau[17] exploring the bottom of the sea, looking around, taking her sweet time. Finally, she chooses a pew,[18] but she wants to sit in the *other* end. It's like she had a spot picked out for some unknown reason, and although it's the most inconvenient seat in the house, that's where she has to sit. So we squeeze by all the people already sitting there, saying, "Excuse me, please, *con permiso*, pardon me," getting annoyed looks the whole way. By the time we settle in, I'm drenched[19] in sweat. I keep my head down like I'm praying so as not to see or be seen. She is praying loud, in Spanish, and singing hymns[20] at the top of her creaky voice.

13   I ignore her when she gets up with a hundred other people to take communion.[21] I'm actually praying hard now—that this will all be over soon. But the next time I look up, I see a black coat dragging around and around the church, stopping here and there so a little gray head can peek out[22] like a periscope on a submarine. There are giggles in the church, and even the priest has frozen in the middle of a blessing,[23] his hands above his head like he is about to lead the congregation[24] in a set of jumping jacks.[25]

14   I realize to my horror that my grandmother is lost. She can't find her way back to the pew. I am so embarrassed that even though the woman next to me is shooting daggers at me[26] with her eyes, I just can't move to get her. I put my hands over my face like I'm praying, but it's really to hide my burning cheeks. I would like for her to disappear. I just know that Monday my friends, and my enemies, in the barrio[27] will have a lot of senile-grandmother jokes to tell in front of me. I am frozen to my seat. So the woman who wants me dead on the spot does it for me. She makes a big deal out of getting up and hurrying to get Abuela.

---

[16]**purgatory** according to Catholic beliefs, the place where dead souls suffer for the bad things they have done before they can enter heaven

[17]**Captain Cousteau** Jacques Cousteau, famous French underwater explorer

[18]**pew** a long wooden seat in a church

[19]**drenched** completely wet

[20]**hymns** religious songs

[21]**take communion** to participate in a particular Christian ceremony

[22]**peek out** to look at something quickly

[23]**blessing** a prayer

[24]**congregation** a group of people attending a religious service

[25]**jumping jacks** an exercise in which you jump and move your arms

[26]**shooting daggers at me** looking at me very angrily

[27]**barrio** *(Spanish)* a neighborhood, especially where many Spanish-speaking people live

15   The rest of the mass is a blur.[28] All I know is that my grandmother kneels the whole time with her hands over *her* face. She doesn't speak to me on the way home, and she doesn't let me help her walk, even though she almost falls a couple of times.

16   When we get to the apartment, my parents are at the kitchen table, where my mother is trying to eat some soup. They can see right away that something is wrong. The Abuela points her finger at me like a judge passing a sentence on a criminal. She says in Spanish, "You made me feel like a zero, like a nothing." Then she goes to her room.

17   I try to explain what happened. "I don't understand why she's so upset. She just got lost and wandered around for a while," I tell them. But it sounds lame, even to my own ears. My mother gives me a look that makes me cringe and goes in to Abuela's room to get her version of the story. She comes out with tears in her eyes.

18   "Your grandmother says to tell you that of all the hurtful things you can do to a person, the worst is to make them feel as if they are worth nothing."

19   I can feel myself shrinking right there in front of her. But I can't bring myself to tell my mother that I think I understand how I made Abuela feel. I might be sent into the old lady's room to apologize, and it's not easy to admit you've been a jerk—at least not right away with everybody watching. So I just sit there not saying anything.

20   My mother looks at me for a long time, like she feels sorry for me. Then she says, "You should know, Constancia, that if it wasn't for this old woman whose existence you don't seem to value, you and I would not be here."

21   That's when *I'm* sent to *my* room to consider a number I hadn't thought much about—until today.

---

[28]**a blur** something difficult to remember

THINKING ABOUT THE STORY

Comprehension

Discuss the following questions as a class.

1. Why does Constancia's grandmother visit the family?
2. What does the grandmother do when she reaches the family's home? How does Constancia feel? How does she react?
3. How does Constancia's father get Constancia to take her grandmother to church?
4. What does the grandmother do in church? How does Constancia feel?
5. How does Constancia act toward her grandmother in the church? How does the grandmother feel?
6. What happens after Constancia and her grandmother get home?
7. How does Constancia feel at the end of the story?

Focus on Reading: Distinguishing Fact from Opinion

> The ability to distinguish fact from opinion is an important reading skill. In general, a *fact* is information that can be proven. Most people believe it is true. In contrast, an *opinion* has not been proven. A person or group of people believes it is true, but it might not be.
>
> For example, the statement *snow is cold* is a fact because it can be proven. However, the statement *snow is beautiful* is an opinion, because only some people believe it is true.

A. Read each statement. Write *F* if it is a fact and *O* if it is an opinion. Then compare answers in small groups.

_____ 1. Abuela is four feet eleven inches tall.

_____ 2. Constancia's parents paid for Abuela's airplane ticket.

_____ 3. The dirty slush in New York is not worth the price of an airplane ticket.

_____ 4. Abuela's soul will be eternally damned if she doesn't go to Sunday mass.

_____ 5. The mass is at ten o'clock on Sunday.

_____ 6. Everyone Constancia ever met was at the mass.

_____ 7. Abuela walks as slow as Captain Cousteau exploring the bottom of the sea.

_____ 8. Abuela sits in the most inconvenient seat in the church.

_____ 9. Abuela gets lost in the church.

_____ 10. The woman sitting next to Constancia in church is angry with her.

_____ 11. The woman sitting next to Constancia wants her dead on the spot.

_____ 12. Abuela doesn't talk to Constancia on the way home from church.

B. Write one more statement of fact and one more opinion statement based on the story.

Focus on Literature: Hyperbole

> Writers sometimes exaggerate facts to create a strong or humorous effect. This is called *hyperbole*. "My aunt always puts a ton of food on my plate" and "My sister is as slow as a snail" are examples of hyperbole.

Work with a partner. Find and underline examples of hyperbole in the story. What facts or details does the author exaggerate? Why do you think she exaggerates them?

Expansion

Discuss the following questions in small groups.

1. What Spanish words does the author use? Why do you think she uses them?
2. Have you ever been in a place where you didn't want to be seen with another family member? If so, explain.
3. Have people ever "shot daggers at you" with their eyes? If so, what were you doing?
4. Her grandmother says, "of all the hurtful things you can do to a person, the worst is to make them feel as if they are worth nothing." Do you agree? Explain.
5. Reread paragraphs 19–21. Why do you think the author chose the title "Abuela Invents the Zero"?
6. What do you think Constancia does after she goes to her room? Explain.

RESPONDING TO THE STORY

Write about one of the following topics.

1. **Feeling Like a Zero.** Write a story about a time when you made someone (or someone made you) feel like a zero. Use the following questions to help you.

   • Where were you?
   • Who was the person?
   • What did you (or the other person) do?
   • How did you (or the other person) react?
   • What happened in the end and what did you learn?

   If appropriate, use hyperbole to exaggerate facts. You can also include some words from another language.

2. **What Happens Next?** What do you think happens after Constancia goes to her room? Does she apologize to Abuela? Does Abuela go back to Puerto Rico without saying goodbye? Write about what happens next. You can use hyperbole to exaggerate facts if appropriate.

3. **An Apology.** Imagine that you are Constancia. Your grandmother has gone back to Puerto Rico. Write a letter to her. Explain why you acted as you did and how you feel about it.

Peer Response

Work with a partner. Exchange papers and read each other's writing. Discuss the following questions.

   • Are there any words from another language? If so, what do they mean?
   • Are there any statements of fact?
   • Are there any opinion statements?
   • Are there any examples of hyperbole? If so, what is exaggerated?
   • Do you have any questions for the writer?
   • What do you like best about the writing?

After you discuss your ideas, you may want to revise your writing.

About the Author

Judith Ortiz Cofer is a native of Puerto Rico, but she grew up mainly in Paterson, New Jersey. She is the author of a novel, two books of poetry, and three collections of prose and poetry. "Abuela Invents the Zero" is from her collection *An Island Like You: Stories from the Barrio. An Island Like You* was selected Best Book of the Year (1995–1996) by the American Library Association and awarded the Pura Belpre medal by REFORMA of ALA. Judith Ortiz Cofer lives in Atlanta, Georgia, where she is a professor of English and creative writing at the University of Georgia.

Blue Stone

SETTING THE CONTEXT

Discussion

Discuss the following questions as a class.

1. When you were a child, did you ever imagine that a certain object had unusual or magical powers? If so, describe the object and its special powers.
2. In the United States, some people believe that carrying a rabbit's foot brings good luck. In your country, do some people believe that carrying a certain object will bring them good luck? If so, what object(s)?

Vocabulary

The boldfaced words in the following sentences are from the poem on page 130. Circle the best definitions for the boldfaced words. Use a dictionary if necessary.

1. Steve acted **indifferent** around Mia so she wouldn't know he liked her.
   a. slightly worried
   b. not interested
   c. very strangely

2. I watched the airplanes **sail** through the sky.
   a. move quickly
   b. stop suddenly
   c. disappear completely

3. Seen from the Earth, a star looks like a **speck** in the sky.
   a. unclear image
   b. large circle
   c. small spot

4. It's easiest to sail a boat **downwind**.
   a. in the same direction as the wind
   b. against the wind
   c. far away from the wind

5. Nothing will **veer** Alex away from his goal of becoming a dentist.
   a. cause to remember
   b. cause to change direction
   c. have no effect on

6. Frank is very **cold**. He never smiles or says "Hello."
   a. friendly
   b. unfriendly
   c. busy

READING THE POEM

In "Blue Stone," the poet describes a special stone with magical qualities. As you read the poem, look for the "magics" that the stone can do. Also, pay attention to the way the poet describes the stone.

Blue Stone

by Richard Hugo

A blue stone is only one piece
of a huge blue stone no one can find.
A blue stone is anything but
a blue stone. It is a speck of sky
5 in your hand or a tiny bit of sea.
Of all stones, it contains
the most magics. It can veer your life
away from poverty to riches. It can grow a tree
exactly where you need shade. Just rub[1]
10 a blue stone and make a wish. A blue stone
becomes the blue marble shooter[2]
you won all those marble games with.
I always act indifferent
around blue stones, sort of nonchalant[3]
15 like I feel they're nothing special.
That way they work best for me.
I avoid cold faces and cruel remarks.
When I sail a blue stone downwind into
the long blue day, armies start marching.
20 When I find the stone, armies stop.
When I sail a blue stone into the wind
that always precedes a rain in Montana
and then find the stone and pick it up
a bird sings blue rain.
25 Days I can't find a blue stone
no matter where I look, I know they've returned
every one to the big blue stone they came from
somewhere in the blue mountains,
somewhere unmapped and roadless
30 that can't be seen from the air.

---

[1]**rub** to move your hand over something while pressing against it

[2]**shooter** a marble you shoot from the hand

[3]**nonchalant** behaving calmly and without interest or worry

THINKING ABOUT THE POEM

Comprehension

Discuss the following questions as a class.

1. Where does the poet say a blue stone comes from?
2. According to the poet, what two things can a blue stone do?
3. How does the poet always act around blue stones? Why?
4. What happens when he sails a blue stone downwind?
5. What happens when he finds the stone?
6. What happens on days he can't find a blue stone?

Focus on Reading: Visualizing

> In Unit 1, you learned that writers use language in special ways to create powerful images. To understand the writer's feelings about a subject, you can *visualize* the images, or try to see them in your mind. For example, in lines 4–5 of "Blue Stone," the words *speck of sky* create a powerful image of the stone's color.

A. Use a word map to help visualize the poem.

1. Underline six strong images of a blue stone that create powerful pictures in your mind (for example, *speck of sky*).
2. Complete the following word map with the images you underlined.

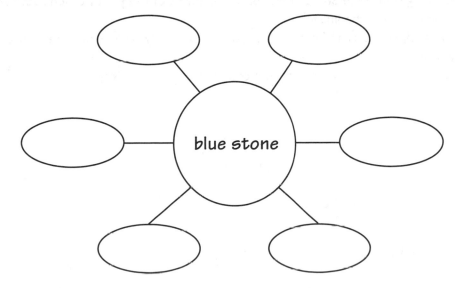

3. Visualize the images in the word map.
4. Read the poem again.

B. Discuss the following questions as a class.

1. Do you notice any similarities among the images? If so, what are they?
2. What do the similarities suggest about the poet's feeling toward the blue stone?
3. How do you think the poet feels toward nature? Why?

Focus on Literature: Fantasy

Fantasy is writing that includes unreal or magical characters, situations, or events. Writers sometimes use fantasy to create delightful and imaginative possibilities for the reader. For example, they may give ordinary objects special powers that are not possible in real life.

Discuss the following questions as a class.

1. What are some examples of fantasy in "Blue Stone"? Underline them.
2. Do you like these examples? If so, which examples do you like best? Why?
3. Does the poet's use of fantasy affect your attitude toward blue stones? If so, how?
4. Do you think fantasy is important to adults as well as children? If so, why?

Expansion

Discuss the following questions in small groups.

1. What images in "Blue Stone" bring back memories of the poet's childhood? Why do you think he uses the images?
2. Did you enjoy books and movies that contained fantasy when you were a child? Why or why not?
3. Do you enjoy books and movies that contain fantasy now? Why or why not?

RESPONDING TO THE POEM

Write about one of the following topics.

1. **An Object Poem.** Using "Blue Stone" as a model, write a poem about an unusual or special object you now own (for example, a stone, shell, or piece of wood). Consider the following questions.

   - Where did you get the object?
   - What is your feeling toward the object? What images do you associate or connect with the object?
   - Do you imagine the object has any special powers?
   - How do you act around the object?

   Use fantasy in your poem if appropriate.

2. **A Special Object.** Write a poem, paragraph, or essay about a toy or other object that was special to you when you were a child. Consider the following questions.

   - Where did you get the object?
   - What images did you associate with the object?
   - Did you ever imagine that it had special powers?
   - How did you feel about the object?
   - How did you act around it?
   - What happened to the object?

   Use fantasy in your poem or paragraph if appropriate.

3. **My Attitude Toward Fantasy.** Write a paragraph or essay explaining your attitude toward fantasy. Use the following questions to help you.

   - Did you like fantasy as a child? Why or why not?
   - Do you like fantasy now? Why or why not?
   - Has your attitude toward fantasy changed since you were a child? If so, how?

Peer Response

Work with a partner. Exchange papers and read each other's writing. Discuss the following questions.

- What is the subject of the writing?
- What is the writer's opinion of the subject? State it in your own words.
- What images are the strongest?
- Does the writer use any examples of fantasy? If so, what are they?
- Do you have any questions for the writer?
- What do you like best about the writing?

After you discuss your ideas, you may want to revise your writing.

About the Author

Richard Hugo (1923–1982) was born near Seattle, Washington. He served as director of the Creative Writing Program at the University of Montana for many years. He received many awards for his poetry, including the Theodore Roethke Memorial Poetry Prize. "Blue Stone" is from *Making Certain It Goes On: The Collected Poems of Richard Hugo*, which includes his other poems about stones: "Red Stone," "Gray Stone," "Green Stone," "Brown Stone," and "Gold Stone."

ON FURTHER REFLECTION

Making Connections

Discuss the following questions.

1. When you were growing up, were you similar to any of the children in Diane Kahanu's poem or to Constancia in Judith Ortiz Cofer's story? If so, which one(s)? How were you similar?
2. Richard Hugo learned to use imagination and fantasy as a child. He continued to use them to write poetry such as "Blue Stone" as an adult. Did you learn anything special as a child that you continue to use now? If so, what did you learn?
3. What did you learn from Deborah Tannen's essay about the different ways boys and girls communicate? How does it relate to your life?

Connecting to Community

Choose one of the following projects.

1. Does your community have any programs that help children? If so, consider volunteering to work for one. Report your experience to the class.
2. One way to relive one's childhood is to spend time with children—especially by reading to them. Spend some time reading to a child in your family or a friend's family. If the child can read, ask him or her to read you a favorite story. Report your experience to the class.
3. Invite an older person to your class. Ask the person to talk about his or her childhood. What are his or her favorite memories? What childhood events have had the most influence on his or her adult life?

Work

Work. How does that word make you feel? Most people spend more time working than doing any other activity. They work to pay for food, shelter, and clothing. But beyond these needs, work gives structure and meaning to people's lives. Some people work as little as possible, while others work so much that work becomes the most important thing in their lives.

Work—its quality, challenges, and demands—is an important subject for the people you will meet in this unit. Poet Martín Espada introduces Jorge, a janitor who quits his job. Playwright Eric Bogosian presents Bottleman, a homeless man who collects bottles and cans for a living. In Gregorio López y Fuentes's short story, a poor farmer named Lencho writes an unusual letter for help—with surprising results. Finally, professor and essayist Johnnetta B. Cole describes how she followed her passion to find an unusual and rewarding career.

Whether you have worked, are working now, or will work in the future, your work will be a major part of your life. As the people in this unit show, your work defines you in many important ways.

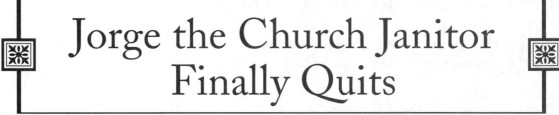

Jorge the Church Janitor Finally Quits

SETTING THE CONTEXT

Discussion

Discuss the following questions as a class.

1. A janitor cleans and takes care of a building. In your country, what kinds of cleaning do janitors do?
2. What kind of people usually work as janitors in your country? Are they men or women? Young or old? From your country or from other countries?
3. How do you view janitors and their work? Why?
4. How do you think janitors view their own work? Why?

READING THE POEM

As you read the poem, think about the way the janitor feels. How long do you think he has felt this way? Why do you think he *finally* quits his job?

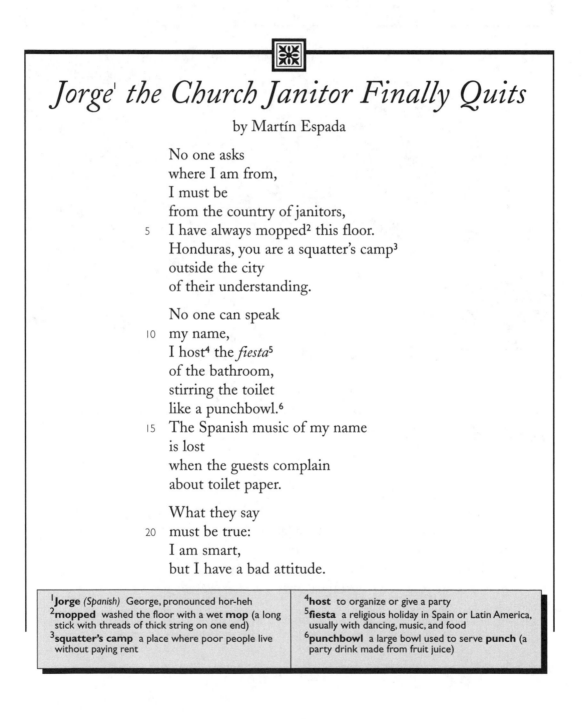

Jorge[1] the Church Janitor Finally Quits

by Martín Espada

No one asks
where I am from,
I must be
from the country of janitors,
5   I have always mopped[2] this floor.
Honduras, you are a squatter's camp[3]
outside the city
of their understanding.

No one can speak
10   my name,
I host[4] the *fiesta*[5]
of the bathroom,
stirring the toilet
like a punchbowl.[6]
15   The Spanish music of my name
is lost
when the guests complain
about toilet paper.

What they say
20   must be true:
I am smart,
but I have a bad attitude.

---

[1]**Jorge** *(Spanish)* George, pronounced hor-heh
[2]**mopped** washed the floor with a wet **mop** (a long stick with threads of thick string on one end)
[3]**squatter's camp** a place where poor people live without paying rent

[4]**host** to organize or give a party
[5]**fiesta** a religious holiday in Spain or Latin America, usually with dancing, music, and food
[6]**punchbowl** a large bowl used to serve **punch** (a party drink made from fruit juice)

No one knows
that I quit tonight,
25   maybe the mop
will push on without me,
sniffing[7] along the floor
like a crazy squid[8]
with stringy[9] gray tentacles.[10]
30   They will call it Jorge.

---

[7]**sniffing** moving like a dog that is smelling the air in search of something
[8]**squid** a sea animal with ten long arms around its mouth

[9]**stringy** long and thin, like string
[10]**tentacles** the arms of a squid

THINKING ABOUT THE POEM

Comprehension

Discuss the following questions as a class.

1. Where is Jorge from?
2. What is his native language? Do you think he speaks English well? Why or why not?
3. Why do you think he says, "No one asks where I am from"?
4. Why do you think he says, "No one can speak my name"?
5. Why do you think he quits his job?
6. How do you think Jorge feels when he quits? Explain.
7. Why do you think the poet uses the word *finally* in the title? What meaning does it express?
8. Underline the similes (comparisons with *like* or *as*) in the second and fourth stanzas of the poem. What two things does the poet compare in each simile? How do these two similes help you understand Jorge's feelings?

Focus on Reading: Pronoun Referents

As you learned in Unit 2, when reading, it is important to know which nouns the pronouns refer to. However, sometimes writers use pronouns that do not refer to specific nouns. In these cases, the pronoun referent is implied; it is not stated directly. For example:

They didn't have penicillin during World War I, so many soldiers died of influenza.

In this example, the pronoun *they* refers to doctors and nurses. The pronoun referent "doctors and nurses" is not stated directly; it is only implied.

A. Read the poem again. Write the referents for the following pronouns on the lines. If the pronoun referent is implied, write the noun you *think* the pronoun refers to. Then compare and discuss your answers. (**Note:** More than one answer may be possible, and some pronouns may refer to the same noun.)

1. no one (line 1) _____

2. their (line 8) _____

3. they (line 19) _____

4. they (line 30) _____

5. it (line 30) _____

B. Why do you think the poet doesn't directly state who *they* and *their* refer to?

Focus on Literature: Dramatic Monologue

A *dramatic monologue* is a form of writing in which one character speaks directly to the reader. Usually, the character gives a monologue because something important has just happened to him or her. The dramatic monologue reveals the character's personality, feelings, and attitudes toward the event in a direct and powerful way.

Discuss the following questions.

1. Why do you think Jorge speaks to the reader? What has just happened?
2. What does the monologue reveal about Jorge's personality?
3. What does the monologue reveal about his feelings and attitude toward his job?
4. How do you think the poet feels about Jorge? Explain.
5. Why do you think the poet wrote this poem as a dramatic monologue?

Expansion

Discuss the following questions in small groups.

1. Have you ever had a job you really disliked? If so, describe the job. If not, what would you do if you had such a job?
2. Have you ever had a job you really liked? If so, describe it. Why did you like it?
3. Have you ever quit something? If so, what did you quit? Why? How did you feel afterward?
4. When do you think quitting something is acceptable? When is it unacceptable? Explain.
5. How important is attitude in determining success? Explain. What other factors can determine success in life?

Responding to the Poem

Write about one of the following topics.

1. **A Dramatic Monologue.** Write a dramatic monologue about a character with a job he or she really likes or dislikes. Use "Jorge the Church Janitor Finally Quits" as a model. Use the following questions and your own experience.

   • Who is the character?
   • What is the character's personality like?
   • What are the character's feelings and attitudes toward the job?
   • What important event has just happened to the character?

2. **Quitting.** Write a poem, paragraph, or essay about a time when you quit something. Use the following questions to help you.

   • Why did you quit?
   • How did you feel when you quit?
   • Do you think quitting was the right thing to do? Why or why not?

3. **Attitude.** Write a poem, paragraph, or essay about an experience in which your attitude contributed to your success or failure. Use the following questions to help you.

   • What were you doing?
   • What was your attitude? Why?
   • How did your attitude contribute to your success or failure?
   • What did you learn?

Peer Response

Work with a partner. Exchange papers and read each other's writing. Discuss the following questions.

- What does the writing reveal about the character's (or writer's) personality?
- What does the writing reveal about the character's (or writer's) feelings and attitudes?
- Do you have any questions for the writer?
- What do you like best about the writing?

After you discuss your ideas, you may want to revise your writing.

About the Author

Martín Espada's books include *The Immigrant Iceboy's Bolero* and *Trumpets from the Island of their Eviction*. In 1986, he was awarded a fellowship from the National Endowment of the Arts. His poems appear in many literary magazines and anthologies, including *An Ear to the Ground: An Anthology of Contemporary American Poetry* and *After Aztlan: Latino Poets of the Nineties*.

Bottleman

SETTING THE CONTEXT

Discussion

Discuss the following questions as a class.

1. Describe the picture. Who is the man? What is he doing?
2. Where do you think this scene takes place?
3. Have you ever observed a scene like this anywhere? Explain.

Vocabulary

The boldfaced idioms in the following sentences are from the play on pages 145–147. Use the context to guess the meanings of the boldfaced words. Use a dictionary if necessary. Then match the boldfaced idioms with the correct definitions that follow. Compare your answers in small groups.

_____ 1. My parents have blue eyes, and so do I. Blue eyes **run in our family**.

_____ 2. People were buying the paintings **like crazy**; after an hour, there were none left.

_____ 3. I don't like opera. It's **not my bag**.

_____ 4. When we found out the concert tickets were $75, I said, "**Forget it**." I didn't want to spend that much money.

_____ 5. When CDs were invented, **that was it** for vinyl records.

_____ 6. I said, "**Come on**! We're going to be late!"

a. not something that interests me
b. that was the end
c. go faster
d. are characteristic of my relatives
e. very quickly
f. it's impossible

READING THE PLAY

"Bottleman" is a monologue—a short play in which only one character speaks to the audience. As you read the play, think about Bottleman's situation. What is his job? Where does he live? What things does he have to live without? What is his attitude toward his work? Toward his life?

Bottleman

by Eric Bogosian

(A man talks quickly, nervously, rarely looking at the audience. He constantly hitches his pants and pats his hair. His over-cheerful manner covers his fear. He's making conversation with an imaginary listener. He begins by talking to the wall.)

1   I don't like to complain. I'm not a complaining kind of guy, I'm a happy kind of guy—runs in my family, happiness. Never been sick in my life. Not one day. Unless you count broken bones, which I don't. But I like to stay positive. Stay on the sunny side of the street. You can give me a pack of cigarettes, egg salad sandwich, cup of coffee, a newspaper, someplace to sit down, and I'm happy—I'm happy.

(Turns, paces, then stops.)

2   I don't even need the cigarettes. I should quit anyway. It's a dirty habit. Unhealthy. Expensive. Of course you can always find cigarettes. People always have cigarettes—they'll give 'em to you. Food's another subject altogether. People aren't exactly walking around with an egg salad sandwich in their pocket—unless they're crazy! And you figure, egg salad sandwich's gonna run you maybe seventy-eighty bottles. I'm findin' maybe fifty bottles a day—you're talking a shortfall[1] of about twenty bottles . . . or cans . . . bottles or cans, it doesn't make much difference.

(Now another direction, paces, stops)

3   Back in the old days, I used to weigh a lot more than I do now. Used to be on a diet all the time. Always trying to lose weight. I don't have that problem anymore. I'm on the egg salad sandwich diet now. One egg salad sandwich every two days . . . you lose weight like crazy. The fat just flies off . . . and it stays off. I'm gonna patent[2] it. Get a copyright[3] and put an ad in the newspaper. Make a little money.

4   See, newspapers—newspapers, you can get. You can always find a newspaper, people just leave 'em around. And I read 'em. I wanna know about the world.

(His pacing has him facing completely upstage, his back to the audience.)

5   It's important to stay informed. I read about a train in Japan goes three hundred miles a hour, gets you there in no time. They got hotels for cockroaches now, hotels for mice. I stay away from hotels. Too much

---

[1] **shortfall** the difference between the amount you have and the amount you need

[2] **patent** a document that allows a person to make or sell a new invention

[3] **copyright** the legal right to make or sell something

money—who's got that kinda money? Ten bucks[4] a night, forget it. You figure that's two hundred bottles—bottles or cans—and that's not in my budget.

(Now he's facing the audience, talking to the audience in a detached way.)

6   But it's not a problem. You can always find someplace—there's always someplace to stay. You wedge[5] yourself in someplace. The real problem is the concrete. The stone. They make everything out of rocks and cement! Too hard. Whatever happened to wood? Used to be all the buildings were made out of wood. Used to make benches outa wood. But no more. Because they make wood outa trees, and trees, they don't got them no more.

7   I saw this tree . . . there was this tree, beautiful tree . . . they dug a hole and put it in the sidewalk. Everyday I come to say hello. And this guy was backing up his truck. The truck was making that beep sound—beep-beep-beep-beep—right over the tree, 'cause, see, the tree can't hear that. See? That was it for the tree. That was it. What are you gonna do? It's just in the nature of a tree that if you run 'em over they die. They're not like people—they can't take the abuse.

8   Take a tree, replace it with a metal pole, then there's no problem. Truck hits the pole, that's it. But you lose the leaves. You lose the leaves and the twigs. You lose the wood. Wood is good.

(Paces, suddenly:)

9   Dogs like wood. I know—I used to have a dog. Walked him every day. I used to say *(miming walking the dog)*: "Come on! Come on! . . . Who takes care of you? Who takes care of you? *I* take care of you . . . Who's gonna take care of *me* in my old age? Who's gonna take care of me?" That's what I used to ask him . . .

10   He ran away. But that's okay—they gotta eat too, the little ones. Everybody's gotta eat, sooner or later. It's human nature.[6] It's human nature. I like to eat. I like to eat. Kind of a habit of mine, food.

(He holds an imaginary sandwich before his face.)

11   Nice egg salad sandwich. Cup a coffee . . . Cream. Sugar.

12   I'm cutting down on the coffee. I don't drink much coffee these days. Sixty cents a cup. Where did they come up with that figure, that's the question I want to ask. Should be ten cents! But they got ya, see, they got ya. 'Cause they got the beans. They got the beans.[7] You got no choice. They got a cartel.[8] This OPEC.[9]

---

[4]**buck** *(informal)* a dollar
[5]**wedge** to push into a small space
[6]**human nature** the usual characteristics of people
[7]**beans** *(in this case)* coffee beans

[8]**cartel** a group of companies that work together to control prices
[9]**OPEC** **O**rganization of **P**etroleum **E**xporting **C**ountries

13   But I don't need coffee. I don't need the coffee. People drink coffee to stay awake—I don't need to stay awake. I'm awake, I'm awake. You gotta keep your eyes open when you're sleeping, 'cause you find a place to lie down and you don't keep your eyes open and a guy comes back with a baseball bat and that's it—*bang bang*, you're dead!

14   No more coffee, no more cigarettes—that's it!

15   See, these guys on the street, they like to fight. I don't got that luxury. I'm on my second set of teeth, I'm missing a kneecap, I can't hear in one ear. I'm like the bionic man[9] without the hardware.[10] I'm no Cassius Clay. I'm no Cassius Clay.[11]

(Pause)

16   But I stay on the sunny side of the street. I stay on the sunny side of the street. A guy once told me, "Life is like a half a glass of water . . . half a glass of water . . . ."

(He loses his train of thought; his hand is shaking, holding the imaginary glass.)

17   "You got a half a glass of water . . . ." And . . . uh . . . "you should drink the water," that's what he said . . . .

(Sheepish—he didn't get the saying right—he turns away, then laughs at himself.)

18   No, that isn't what he said . . . . He said . . . he said . . . "Half a glass a water is better than no water at all!" That's it. "Half a glass a water is better than no water . . . ."

(Full of energy again)

19   I look at it this way—I could be living in Ethiopia. Those poor people got it terrible. They got nothing to eat. Starving all the time. They just sit in the sand all day long . . . . It's too sunny, too many flies . . . it's not for me. It's not my bag. I prefer it here . . . it's better here.

(Lost in thought, convincing himself)

20   It's good here, it's good. It's good. Thank God!

(Pause. He's just standing, staring at the ground.)

(He snaps out of it—sunny, cheerful again, he addresses the audience.)

21   Well, I gotta get going, got to get to work. You know what they say: "The early bird catches the can!"

22   Or bottles . . . bottles or cans, it don't make no difference . . . .

(He walks off upstage, still talking.)

23   It don't make no difference at all . . . .

---

[9]**bionic man** *(from a 1970s TV show)* a man who was given robot parts after an injury
[10]**hardware** metal machine or computer parts

[11]**Cassius Clay** boxer Muhammed Ali's original name

THINKING ABOUT THE PLAY

Comprehension

Discuss the following questions as a class.

1. What five things does Bottleman say he needs to be happy?
2. What is easy for him to get? What is difficult for him to get?
3. How does he get information about the world?
4. Why does he stay away from hotels? Where do you think he sleeps?
5. Why does he prefer wood to concrete?
6. Bottleman mentions three sayings, or proverbs:

   - "I stay on the sunny side of the street." (paragraph 16)
   - "Half a glass of water is better than no water." (paragraph 18)
   - "The early bird catches the can." (an adaptation of the saying "The early bird catches the worm," paragraph 21)

What do these sayings mean? What do they show about Bottleman's attitude toward life?

Focus on Reading: Reduced Forms

> As you learned in Unit 3, writers use *reduced forms* to make their characters' speech sound natural. For example, they may run two or more words together so it sounds like one word. Eric Bogosian uses reduced forms to make Bottleman's speech sound conversational.

Work with a partner. Read the following sentences from the play. The boldfaced words are reduced forms. Rewrite the sentences using complete, grammatically correct forms.

1. They **gotta** eat too.

   They've got to eat too.

2. Who's **gonna** take care of me?

   _____

3. I **wanna** know about the world.

   _____

4. Who's got that **kinda** money?

_____

5. Used to make benches **outa** wood.

_____

Focus on Literature: Characterization

> Writers create different kinds of characters for different purposes. This is called *characterization*.
>
> Writers may create *flat* and *round* characters. *Flat characters* usually represent a specific quality, such as good, evil, kindness, or cruelty. These characters have little or no complexity beyond their one specific quality. In contrast, *round characters* are more complex. They usually have several qualities, some of which are contradictory and surprising.
>
> Writers also create *sympathetic* and *unsympathetic* characters. *Sympathetic characters* have motivations and feelings that the reader can understand. *Unsympathetic characters* have motivations and feelings that the reader cannot understand. We often say that we can identify with a sympathetic character, but not with an unsympathetic character.

Discuss the following questions with a partner.

1. Describe Bottleman. Do you think he is a flat or a round character? Why?
2. Do you think he is a sympathetic or unsympathetic character? Why?

Expansion

Discuss the following questions in small groups.

1. At the beginning of the monologue, Bottleman says, "I'm happy—I'm happy." Do you believe him? Explain.
2. What do you think Bottleman used to do when he was younger? Why?
3. If you met Bottleman on the street, how would you react? Why?
4. If you were homeless, where do you think you would sleep? What would you eat? How would you get money?

RESPONDING TO THE PLAY

Write about one of the following topics.

1. **Backstory.** As you learned in Unit 3, actors sometimes create backstory, or short biographies for their characters, to help them play them more realistically. Imagine that you are an actor who is going to play Bottleman. Write backstory for him. Use the following questions and your own ideas.

   - What is his real name?
   - How old is he?
   - Where is his family?
   - What does he look like?
   - What did he do before he became Bottleman?

2. **Interview.** Imagine that you are a newspaper reporter. Write an interview with Bottleman. First, write questions to ask him. Consider your audience and purpose. What do your readers want to know about him? What do you want to tell your readers? Then write Bottleman's answers. Try to make Bottleman sound like he does in the play. You might begin as follows.

   YOU: Thank you very much for doing this interview.

   BOTTLEMAN: Happy to do it. I'm a happy guy—I'm happy. It's good to be here.

3. **A Monologue.** Imagine you are a person from your city or town, or invent a new character, and write a monologue as if you were that person. Talk to your reader/audience about yourself. Make your speech as natural as possible, using reduced forms if appropriate. Consider these questions:

   - Is your character flat or round? Sympathetic or unsympathetic?
   - What is your character's attitude toward his life and work?
   - Does your character have any sayings to describe this attitude?

   If you wish, perform your monologue for the class.

Peer Response

Work with a partner. Exchange papers and read each other's writing. Discuss the following questions.

- Are there any reduced forms?
- What characters are featured? Describe them.
- Do you have any questions for the writer?
- What do you like best about the writing?

After you discuss your ideas, you may want to revise your writing.

About the Author

Eric Bogosian is an author and actor. He lives and works in New York City. He wrote and performed in the play *Talk Radio*. Later, he starred in the film version, which was directed by Oliver Stone. "Bottleman" is from his play *Sex, Drugs, Rock & Roll*.

A Letter to God

SETTING THE CONTEXT

Discussion

Discuss the following questions as a class.

1. Is farming important in your country? If so, what kinds of crops do farmers grow?
2. Do farmers in your country make much money? Why or why not?
3. What special problems do farmers face? What do they need in order to be successful?
4. What do people think of the post office in your country? Do they ever complain about the service or workers? If so, what do they say?

Vocabulary

The boldfaced words in the following sentences are from the story on pages 154–156. Use the context to guess the meanings of the boldfaced words. Use a dictionary if necessary. Then match the boldfaced words with the correct definitions that follow. Compare your answers in small groups.

_____ 1. We walked up the hill; at the **crest**, we looked down at the town and river below.

_____ 2. The farmer kept his cows in a **corral** so they wouldn't run away.

_____ 3. Don't eat fruit or vegetables before they are **ripe**.

_____ 4. Farmers always hope for a good **harvest**.

_____ 5. We know the Smiths **intimately**; we've been friends with them for years.

_____ 6. John really **resembles** his father; they have a very similar appearance.

_____ 7. I use a computer for all my **correspondence**.

_____ 8. The **crooks** robbed the bank last night.

_____ 9. Money doesn't always bring **contentment**; some rich people are very unhappy.

_____ 10. Melissa has **confidence** in herself. She always thinks she will do well.

a. closely, in a familiar way
b. belief in your own or someone else's ability
c. thieves
d. top, highest point
e. looks like
f. satisfaction
g. fully grown and ready to eat
h. amount of fruits and vegetables gathered
i. letters or notes
j. enclosed area for animals

READING THE STORY

Think about the title of the story. Why might someone write a letter to God? What kind of person might do this?

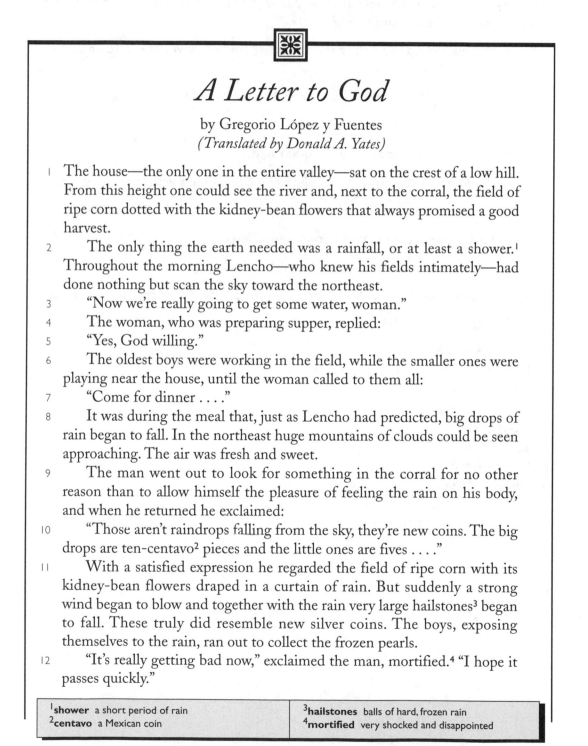

A Letter to God

by Gregorio López y Fuentes
(Translated by Donald A. Yates)

1   The house—the only one in the entire valley—sat on the crest of a low hill. From this height one could see the river and, next to the corral, the field of ripe corn dotted with the kidney-bean flowers that always promised a good harvest.

2   The only thing the earth needed was a rainfall, or at least a shower.[1] Throughout the morning Lencho—who knew his fields intimately—had done nothing but scan the sky toward the northeast.

3   "Now we're really going to get some water, woman."

4   The woman, who was preparing supper, replied:

5   "Yes, God willing."

6   The oldest boys were working in the field, while the smaller ones were playing near the house, until the woman called to them all:

7   "Come for dinner . . . ."

8   It was during the meal that, just as Lencho had predicted, big drops of rain began to fall. In the northeast huge mountains of clouds could be seen approaching. The air was fresh and sweet.

9   The man went out to look for something in the corral for no other reason than to allow himself the pleasure of feeling the rain on his body, and when he returned he exclaimed:

10   "Those aren't raindrops falling from the sky, they're new coins. The big drops are ten-centavo[2] pieces and the little ones are fives . . . ."

11   With a satisfied expression he regarded the field of ripe corn with its kidney-bean flowers draped in a curtain of rain. But suddenly a strong wind began to blow and together with the rain very large hailstones[3] began to fall. These truly did resemble new silver coins. The boys, exposing themselves to the rain, ran out to collect the frozen pearls.

12   "It's really getting bad now," exclaimed the man, mortified.[4] "I hope it passes quickly."

---

[1] **shower** a short period of rain
[2] **centavo** a Mexican coin

[3] **hailstones** balls of hard, frozen rain
[4] **mortified** very shocked and disappointed

13   It did not pass quickly. For an hour the hail rained on the house, the garden, the hillside, the cornfield, on the whole valley. The field was white, as if covered with salt. Not a leaf remained on the trees. The corn was totally destroyed. The flowers were gone from the kidney-bean plants. Lencho's soul[5] was filled with sadness. When the storm had passed, he stood in the middle of the field and said to his sons:

14   "A plague of locusts[6] would have left more than this . . . . The hail has left nothing: this year we will have no corn or beans . . . ."

15   That night was a sorrowful one:

16   "All our work for nothing!"

17   "There's no one who can help us!"

18   "We'll all go hungry this year . . . ."

19   But in the hearts of all who lived in that solitary[7] house in the middle of the valley, there was a single hope: help from God.

20   "Don't be so upset, even though this seems like a total loss. Remember, no one dies of hunger!"

21   "That's what they say: no one dies of hunger . . . ."

22   All through the night, Lencho thought only of his one hope: the help of God, whose eyes, as he had been instructed, see everything, even what is deep in one's conscience.[8]

23   Lencho was an ox[9] of a man, working like an animal in the fields, but still he knew how to write. The following Sunday, at daybreak, after having convinced himself that there is a protecting spirit, he began to write a letter which he himself would carry to town and place in the mail.

24   It was nothing less than a letter to God.

25   "God," he wrote, "if you don't help me, my family and I will go hungry this year. I need a hundred pesos[10] in order to resow[11] the field and to live until the crop comes, because the hailstorm . . . ."

26   He wrote "To God" on the envelope, put the letter inside and, still troubled, went to town. At the post office he placed a stamp on the letter and dropped it into the mailbox.

27   One of the employees, who was a postman and also helped at the post office, went to his boss laughing heartily and showed him the letter to God. Never in his career as a postman had he known that address. The postmaster—a fat, amiable[12] fellow—also broke out laughing, but almost immediately he turned serious and, tapping the letter on his desk, commented:

---

[5]**soul** spirit
[6]**plague of locusts** a large number of insects that destroy crops
[7]**solitary** lonely
[8]**conscience** sense of right and wrong

[9]**ox** a large, strong animal in the cow family; used for farm work
[10]**pesos** Mexican money (100 centavos = 1 peso)
[11]**resow** to plant fruits and vegetables again
[12]**amiable** friendly, pleasant

28   "What faith! I wish I had the faith[13] of the man who wrote this letter. To believe the way he believes. To hope with the confidence that he knows how to hope with. Starting up a correspondence with God!"

29   So, in order not to disillusion[14] that prodigy[15] of faith, revealed by a letter that could not be delivered, the postmaster came up with an idea: answer the letter. But when he opened it, it was evident that to answer it he needed something more than goodwill, ink, and paper. But he stuck to his resolution:[16] he asked for money from his employee, he himself gave part of his salary, and several friends of his were obliged[17] to give something "for an act of charity."[18]

30   It was impossible for him to gather together the hundred pesos, so he was able to send the farmer only a little more than half. He put the bills[19] in an envelope addressed to Lencho and with them a letter containing only a single word as a signature: GOD.

31   The following Sunday Lencho came a bit earlier than usual to ask if there was a letter for him. It was the postman himself who handed the letter to him, while the postmaster, experiencing the contentment of a man who has performed a good deed,[20] looked on from the doorway of his office.

32   Lencho showed not the slightest surprise on seeing the bills—such was his confidence—but he became angry when he counted the money . . . . God could not have made a mistake, nor could he have denied Lencho what he had requested!

33   Immediately, Lencho went up to the window to ask for paper and ink. On the public writing table, he started in to write, with much wrinkling of his brow,[21] caused by the effort he had to make to express his ideas. When he finished, he went to the window to buy a stamp which he licked and then affixed[22] to the envelope with a blow of his fist.

34   The moment that the letter fell into the mailbox the postmaster went to open it. It said:

35   "God: of the money that I asked for, only seventy pesos reached me. Send me the rest, since I need it very much. But don't send it to me through the mail, because the post-office employees are a bunch of crooks. Lencho."

[13]**faith** belief and trust in God
[14]**disillusion** to take away someone's belief or faith
[15]**prodigy** a person with a special ability
[16]**stuck to his resolution** did what he had promised or decided
[17]**were obliged to** felt that it was necessary to

[18]**act of charity** a generous and helpful action
[19]**bills** paper money
[20]**deed** an action
[21]**wrinkling of his brow** moving his forehead so there are lines on it, usually because worried
[22]**affixed** attached

THINKING ABOUT THE STORY

Comprehension

Discuss the following questions as a class.

1. Describe Lencho's farm at the beginning of the story. What does it need?
2. What weather does Lencho predict at the beginning of the story? What happens?
3. Lencho describes the rain with the metaphor: "Those aren't raindrops falling from the sky, they're new coins." Why do you think he says this?
4. The author describes Lencho with the metaphor: "Lencho was an ox of a man." In what ways do you think Lencho was like an ox?
5. Why does Lencho write a letter to God? What does he ask for?
6. What does the postmaster do? Why?
7. How does Lencho feel at the end of the story? Why?
8. What does Lencho do at the end of the story? Why?

Focus on Literature: Dramatic Irony

As you learned in Unit 2, *verbal irony* occurs when a writer or character says the opposite of what he or she means. Another type of irony occurs when the readers know something that a character doesn't know. This type of irony is called *dramatic irony*. An example of dramatic irony occurs in William Shakespeare's play *Romeo and Juliet*. The character Romeo thinks that Juliet is dead, but the readers know that she isn't dead, only asleep. As a result, the readers have a better understanding of the character—or of the character's situation—than the character does.

Discuss the following questions as a class.

1. What did Lencho think about the missing money?
2. As the reader, what do you know really happened to the money?
3. Where in the story does the dramatic irony occur?
4. Does the irony give you a better understanding of Lencho (or his situation) than he has? Explain.
5. How did the author's use of dramatic irony make you feel?

Focus on Reading: Inferring a Moral

As you learned in Unit 3, a *moral* is a practical lesson about life that occurs at the end of some stories. Often, the moral is directly stated. However, sometimes the writer only suggests a lesson about life, through events in the story. The reader must infer the writer's moral, based on the information given.

Discuss the following questions as a class.

1. How does the story end?
2. What was most powerful about the ending?
3. What lesson do you think the author is trying to teach?
4. Do you think this lesson would be more or less powerful if the author stated it directly? Explain.

Expansion

Discuss the following questions in small groups.

1. What do you think of the postmaster's act of charity? Would you have done the same thing? Explain.
2. Have you ever given or done something "for an act of charity" (for example, helping poor people)? If so, describe the experience. What did it teach you?
3. Have you ever thought someone was dishonest, when in fact that person really was honest? If so, describe the experience. What did you learn?

RESPONDING TO THE STORY

Write about one of the following topics.

1. **What Happens Next?** "A Letter to God" has an unexpected, ironic ending. What do you think happens next? What will the postmaster and the other workers do? What will Lencho do? Write a continuation of the story. Use your imagination.

2. **An Act of Kindness.** The postmaster helped Lencho without telling him and without expecting anything in return. The story suggests that ordinary people will do acts of kindness secretly and unexpectedly. Write about an unexpected act of kindness. Use the following questions to help you.

   • Who did the act of kindness?
   • What did the person do?

- Was the act of kindness done secretly?
- What was the response to the person's act?
- What did you learn from this experience?

3. **False Assumptions.** An *assumption* is something you believe is true, although you have no proof. In the story, Lencho makes the false assumption that the post office employees are crooks. Write about a time when you made a false assumption about someone. Use the following questions to help you.

- What did you assume?
- Why did you make this assumption?
- When did you realize your mistake?
- Did you say anything to the person? If so, what did you say? How did the person respond?
- What did you learn from this experience?

Peer Response

Work with a partner. Exchange papers and read each other's writing. Discuss the following questions.

- Do you think the writer is trying to teach a lesson? If so, what is it?
- Is there anything ironic in the situation described? If so, what is it?
- Do you have any questions for the writer?
- What do you like best about the writing?

After you discuss your ideas, you may want to revise your writing.

About the Author

Gregorio López y Fuentes (1895–1966) was a Mexican poet, novelist, and journalist. In 1935, he won the National Prize of Mexico for his novel *El Indio*. His story "A Letter to God" appears in the anthology *Great Short Stories of the World*.

Follow Your Passion

SETTING THE CONTEXT

Discussion

Discuss the following questions as a class.

1. What person has most influenced you in your life? Why?
2. Has anyone ever advised you to pursue a specific career? If so, did you listen to the advice? Explain.
3. Has anyone ever advised you *not* to pursue a specific career? If so, did you listen to the advice? Explain.

Vocabulary

The boldfaced words and expressions in the following sentences are from the essay on pages 162–165. Use the context to guess the meanings of the boldfaced words. Use a dictionary if necessary. Then match the boldfaced words with the correct definitions that follow. Compare your answers in small groups.

_____ 1. Now that Peter has left, Fred is **assuming** the presidency of the company.

_____ 2. Teaching **entails** a lot of preparation and grading.

_____ 3. Jorge **got a kick out of** the movie; he thought it was really funny.

_____ 4. Reading my friend's novel was a **revelation**—I never knew she wrote so well.

_____ 5. Marjorie is determined to **carry out** her dream of becoming a professor.

_____ 6. Many teenagers **idolize** famous pop singers. They love to listen to their music and try hard to see them in concert.

_____ 7. The murderer would not **confess** to the crime, even though the police had strong evidence.

_____ 8. I **cherish** the ring my husband gave me. I take care of it and wear it on special occasions.

_____ 9. The firefighters worked for hours without **ceasing**, even though they were very tired.

_____ 10. Tina's parents laughed **outright** at her silly suggestion, and then they noticed her sad reaction.

_____ 11. It's a **shame** when people lose good opportunities to improve their lives.

_____ 12. High school graduates face many **dilemmas**, such as whether to go to college or to work.

a. something surprising that is suddenly made known
b. stopping
c. admit something
d. without trying to hide one's feelings
e. really enjoyed
f. difficult choices
g. starting an important job
h. involves, requires
i. treasure or value (something)
j. admire or adore (someone)
k. do something that must be organized and planned
l. a disappointing situation

READING THE ESSAY

Your *passion* is what you enjoy doing the most. As you read the essay, think about the title. How did the author find and follow her passion? Who helped her?

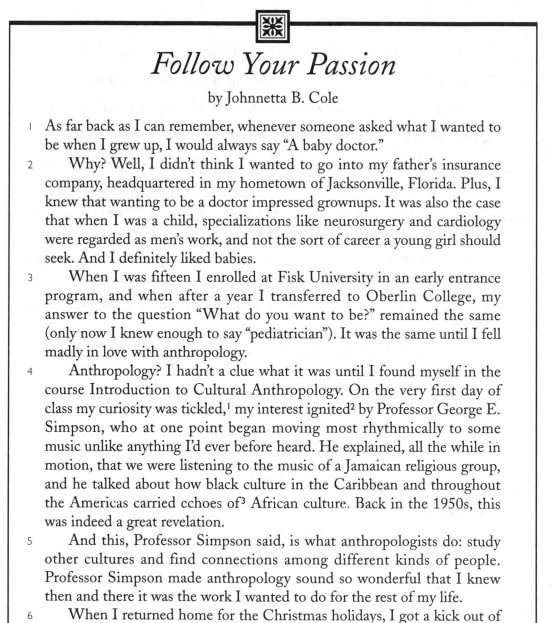

Follow Your Passion

by Johnnetta B. Cole

1   As far back as I can remember, whenever someone asked what I wanted to be when I grew up, I would always say "A baby doctor."

2   Why? Well, I didn't think I wanted to go into my father's insurance company, headquartered in my hometown of Jacksonville, Florida. Plus, I knew that wanting to be a doctor impressed grownups. It was also the case that when I was a child, specializations like neurosurgery and cardiology were regarded as men's work, and not the sort of career a young girl should seek. And I definitely liked babies.

3   When I was fifteen I enrolled at Fisk University in an early entrance program, and when after a year I transferred to Oberlin College, my answer to the question "What do you want to be?" remained the same (only now I knew enough to say "pediatrician"). It was the same until I fell madly in love with anthropology.

4   Anthropology? I hadn't a clue what it was until I found myself in the course Introduction to Cultural Anthropology. On the very first day of class my curiosity was tickled,[1] my interest ignited[2] by Professor George E. Simpson, who at one point began moving most rhythmically to some music unlike anything I'd ever before heard. He explained, all the while in motion, that we were listening to the music of a Jamaican religious group, and he talked about how black culture in the Caribbean and throughout the Americas carried echoes of[3] African culture. Back in the 1950s, this was indeed a great revelation.

5   And this, Professor Simpson said, is what anthropologists do: study other cultures and find connections among different kinds of people. Professor Simpson made anthropology sound so wonderful that I knew then and there it was the work I wanted to do for the rest of my life.

6   When I returned home for the Christmas holidays, I got a kick out of telling folks that I was majoring in anthropology.

---

[1] **my curiosity was tickled** I became curious
[2] **ignited** started

[3] **carried echoes of** had similarities to

7   "What's *that?*" was inevitably[4] the response, and I got a kick out of people's expressions of astonishment[5] as I explained what my newfound passion was all about. "Anthropology is the study of all of humankind," I would say in a very proper voice. "There are four kinds of anthropology: cultural, physical, archaeology, and linguistics. I'm going to be a cultural anthropologist—that is, the kind that studies living people in distant lands and those who live right next door to you. Physical anthropologists study our relationship to other animals, especially primates, and how we humans are as physical beings. Archaeologists study early cultures by digging up remains from the earth. And linguists study different languages all over the world." Once I finished my "rap"[6] on anthropology, people would say, "Oh, I see!"

8   I went about feeling quite pleased and impressed with myself, until the day I talked with my grandfather, whom I idolized and whose approval had always been important to me. Like others, immediately he asked, "What's *that?*"

9   After I explained it, not only was my grandfather not impressed, but he also laughed outright and asked: "And how in the world are you ever going to make a living doing something like that?"

10   My response? I broke into tears[7] and ran for comfort to my mother.

11   Like my grandfather, my mother had questioned my ability to support myself as an anthropologist. However, on this day she gave me some of the best advice I have ever received. Her words were strong and clear: "If you do work that you hate, you will be miserable for the rest of your life. If this is your passion, then follow it."

12   I did, and being an anthropologist, though often a struggle and fraught with[8] uncertainties, has been a source of great emotional and intellectual riches, and a source of satisfaction and fun—as I carried out fieldwork[9] in a black church in Chicago for my master's degree . . . and in Liberia for two years for my Ph.D . . . and later in Cuba, Haiti, the Dominican Republic, St. Croix, and other Caribbean nations. In each of these places I was especially interested in the lives of women. I also focused on issues of race and ethnicity in those Caribbean countries. As I went about learning of various cultures and traditions, I sometimes thought about the difference between the "roughing it"[10] that my work so often entailed and how truly rough[11] it would have been to be engaged in work I really didn't care about.

---

[4]**inevitably** predictably
[5]**astonishment** great surprise
[6]**rap** *(slang)* conversation or talk
[7]**broke into tears** began to cry

[8]**fraught with** full of something bad, such as problems
[9]**fieldwork** research done outside the classroom
[10]**roughing it** living in uncomfortable conditions
[11]**rough** difficult

13   How I wish my grandfather had lived to see the extent[12] to which I did indeed find a way to support myself. For some thirty years I taught anthropology courses to college students, never ceasing to be genuinely happy every time I entered a classroom and began the exciting process of teaching and learning (for teachers must constantly learn, too!). And writing articles and books in the field of anthropology has also been a great source of joy for me, despite the hard work involved in preparing material for publication.

14   In the late 1980s the possibility of a career change came into view. To my great surprise, I was informed one day that I was being considered for the presidency of Spelman College in Atlanta, Georgia. Heading up[13] a college had never been in my dreams, but Spelman had a special significance for me as an African-American woman, because it is the oldest and one of only two historically black colleges for women. And so I followed my heart.

15   How fortunate I was that in assuming the presidency of Spelman, I did not have to totally give up being an anthropologist. While there, I taught one course in my field every spring semester—except in 1996 when I took a course taught by Mary Catherine Bateson.

16   Another good fortune was the countless occasions to counsel[14] students about their majors and career goals, their doubts and dilemmas.

17   "I love psychology, but my dad says I should major in political science," one student confided.

18   "Mom wants me to become a dentist like she is, but I want to be an oceanographer," another one lamented.[15]

19   For yet another it was: "My parents want me to be a doctor, but I want to be a poet."

20   "What should I do?" they all asked.

21   Always my answer was the same: "Follow your passion."

22   I asked these students to think about how it would feel getting up every morning, day in and day out, to face work that they do not like. I reminded them that for so very long women were prohibited[16] from pursuing many kinds of jobs, and that many people in the world have few options when it comes to what they can do to make a living. Isn't it a shame, I would point out, for someone who has the luxury[17] of options,[18] not to explore them?

23   And to the student who confessed that her main motivation for choosing a particular profession was because it paid big money, I told her in

---

[12]**extent** degree, limit
[13]**head up** to lead
[14]**counsel** to advise
[15]**lamented** expressed sadness

[16]**prohibited** not allowed
[17]**luxury** advantage or benefit
[18]**options** choices

a strong and clear voice that just focusing on making a good living can end up meaning not having a very good life, because a lot of money (and the things it can buy) can never truly satisfy the soul.

24   I believe that deep down most people know what they want to be and need to be at a very early age. It shows often in the subjects you like most. It shows in the things you do for fun. But what if you can't name your passion? Well, you could always talk with your parents or teachers about your interests and talents and ask them what kinds of jobs make a good match.

25   If you know your passion, cherish it, nurture it, let it grow. If you're not so sure, don't worry. Just stay open and curious, and in time it will make itself known to you.

THINKING ABOUT THE ESSAY

Comprehension

Discuss the following questions as a class.

1. What did the author want to be when she was young? Why?
2. When did she fall madly in love with anthropology?
3. Why did this subject interest her?
4. Who advised her not to be an anthropologist? Why?
5. What did her mother advise her to do? Why?
6. What does she think about her mother's advice? How do you know?
7. How does she feel about her decision today?
8. What advice does she give her students at Spelman College?

Focus on Reading: Theme

The *theme* of an essay is the writer's main idea about a subject. For example, if the subject is work, the writer's theme might be "work affects your family life" or "where you live affects your work options." Sometimes the writer states the theme directly by using a specific statement or quote. Sometimes the writer implies the theme. In this case, the reader must infer the theme by looking at the events and examples in the essay.

Discuss the following questions as a class.

1. What do you think the author's theme is?
2. What statements in the essay best express the theme?
3. Does the author state or imply the theme? Why do you think she does this?
4. The theme of the essay is not new. Read the following quote from a text that scholars believe is almost 2,000 years old.

   If you bring forth what is within you, then what you bring forth will save you. If you do not bring forth what is within you, what you do not bring forth will destroy you. (Quoted in *The Gnostic Gospels* by Elaine Pagels.)

   How does this message compare with the message in Johnnetta Cole's essay?

Focus on Literature: Motif

A *motif* is a phrase, idea, or image that is frequently repeated in a piece of writing. The motif usually indicates the writer's theme. For example, in the essay "Getups" in Unit 3, Maya Angelou repeats the idea of being true to yourself. She uses this motif to illustrate her thesis about clothes.

Discuss the following questions as a class.

1. What phrase is frequently repeated throughout the essay? How many times does it appear?
2. Why do you think the author uses this motif?
3. Is there a phrase like this in your native language? If so, share it with your classmates.

Expansion

A. What features are important to you in a job? Rank the following features from 1 (most important) to 10 (least important). Compare and discuss your ideas in small groups.

_____ salary   _____ creativity

_____ opportunity to use knowledge or training   _____ working as a team

_____ opportunity to help others   _____ regular hours

_____ opportunity for advancement or promotion   _____ status and power

_____ pleasant surroundings   _____ independence

B. Discuss the following questions in small groups.

1. In paragraph 23, the author says, "just focusing on making a good living can end up meaning not having a very good life, because a lot of money (and the things it can buy) can never truly satisfy the soul." Do you agree or disagree? Explain.

2. In paragraph 24, the author says, "I believe that deep down most people know what they want to be and need to be at a very early age." Do you agree or disagree? Explain.

3. What do you think of the advice "follow your passion"? Can you follow this advice?

RESPONDING TO THE ESSAY

Write about one of the following topics.

1. **Finding Your Passion.** What work will bring you the greatest joy? Write a paragraph or essay describing how you found your passion (or how you hope to find it). Use the following questions to help you.

   • Do you know what work you want to do? If so, how did you find it? If not, how can you find it?
   • Has anyone encouraged or discouraged you about pursuing a specific career? If so, describe the person and your response.
   • Do you plan to "follow your passion"? If so, how?

2. **A Special Person.** In "Follow Your Passion," Johnnetta B. Cole describes a special teacher who greatly influenced her life. Write about a person who greatly influenced your life. Describe the person and how he or she influenced you.

3. **Good Advice.** What is the best advice you have ever received? Write about the advice and the person who gave it to you.

Peer Response

Work with a partner. Exchange papers and read each other's writing. Discuss the following questions.

   • What is the writer's theme?
   • Is a motif repeated throughout the writing? If so, what is it?
   • What did you learn about the writer?
   • Do you have any questions for the writer?
   • What do you like best about the writing?

After you discuss your ideas, you may want to revise your writing.

About the Author

Johnnetta B. Cole was president of Spelman College from 1987 to 1997. In 1998, she began a new job at Emory University as Presidential Distinguished Professor of Anthropology, Women's Studies and African American Studies. Her books include *Conversations: Straight Talk with America's Sister President* and *Dream the Boldest Dreams: And Other Lessons of Life*. She is also the editor of three textbooks: *Anthropology for the Eighties*, *Anthropology for the Nineties*, and *All American Women: Lines That Divide, Ties That Bind*.

ON FURTHER REFLECTION

Making Connections

Discuss the following topics.

1. Which character, Jorge the janitor or Bottleman, do you think has the best chance of changing his life? Why?
2. Imagine that Jorge, Bottleman, and Lencho are new students at Johnnetta B. Cole's college, and that she is their student counselor. What advice do you think she would give each of them? Why?
3. Rank the following people's attitudes toward work from 1 (most positive) to 4 (most negative). Compare and explain your choices.

____ Jorge

____ Bottleman

____ Lencho

____ Johnnetta B. Cole

Connecting to the Community

Choose one of the following projects.

1. Bring the classified ads from the local newspaper to class. Discuss the types of jobs available in your city or town and what qualifications each job requires.
2. Invite someone from an employment office to speak to your class. Ask this person about work opportunities in your school and community.
3. Interview someone in the community who works at a job that you are interested in. Ask about the job and the job qualifications. If possible, visit the person at his or her workplace. Report your findings to the class.

Life and Death

*H*uman beings are perhaps unique among all other living things in their knowledge of life and death. The reality of death has a way of putting life in question. If we are born to die, what is the purpose of life? Does life have meaning and value in itself? Do we give meaning and value to life through our acts—by what we choose to do and *not* do with our lives?

The writers in this unit explore the relationship between life and death. First, Hernando Téllez asks if it is ever acceptable for one person to kill another. Writer William Maxwell reflects on his life as he approaches his ninetieth birthday. Maria Testa shows how a careless act makes some teenagers question their immortality. Finally, poet N. Scott Momady sings a song expressing his appreciation of all living things.

These writers remind us that life is happening *now*—that life presents us, every day, with choices of how to live or die.

Just Lather, That's All

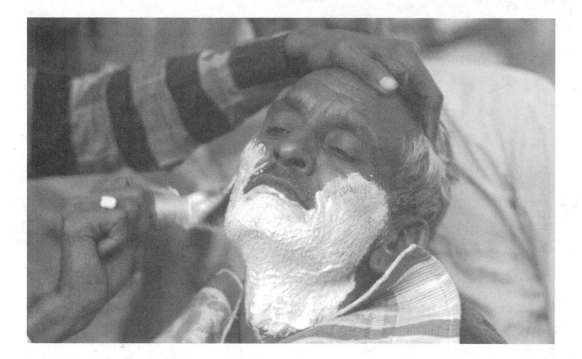

SETTING THE CONTEXT

Discussion

Discuss the following questions as a class.

1. What is happening in the picture?
2. Describe the kind of person who might go to a barber for a shave. Might he be rich, poor, or middle-class? What kind of work might he do?
3. What special skills are required to work as a barber?
4. Is this work dangerous? Explain.

Vocabulary

A. The words in Lists A and B are from the story on pages 173–177. Work with a partner. Match the words with similar meanings. Use a dictionary if necessary.

	List A	List B
_____	1. expedition	a. customer
_____	2. rebels	b. work
_____	3. slit	c. hide
_____	4. taking pains	d. soft
_____	5. client	e. excursion
_____	6. tender	f. conscientious
_____	7. services	g. group
_____	8. executioner	h. revolutionaries
_____	9. faction	i. cut
_____	10. conceal	j. murderer

B. Complete each sentence with the correct word from List A above.

1. The _____ fought the government for many years, but they never won.

2. The tourists went on an _____ to the lost city of Machu Picchu.

3. The children _____ the paper with scissors.

4. To succeed in sales, you need to take care of every _____'s needs.

5. Rachel tries to _____ her emotions, but her feelings always show.

6. Kyle is always _____ with his work; he likes to do a good job.

7. One _____ in the government disagrees with the president's decision.

8. The king ordered the _____ to kill the prisoners.

9. A baby's skin is very _____.

10. The mechanic fixed my car, and I paid him for his _____.

READING THE STORY

Focus on Reading: Making Predictions

An important reading skill is *making predictions*. As you read, you can predict what a character will do next, based on what you already know about the character and his or her situation. Then, as you read further, you can check your predictions—to confirm them or revise them if incorrect. Predicting makes you an active reader: It makes you involved with the characters and interested in how the story will end.

In "Just Lather, That's All," a character faces a terrible dilemma, which causes him great emotional stress. The author builds the action in the story slowly and carefully, so that we experience the character's dilemma—and stress—step by step. The story has been divided into four parts. Before you read each part, make predictions about what will happen next. Then continue reading and revise your predictions if needed.

As you read, think about the two characters. What is their relationship? How do they feel toward each other? Does their attitude toward each other change by the end of the story?

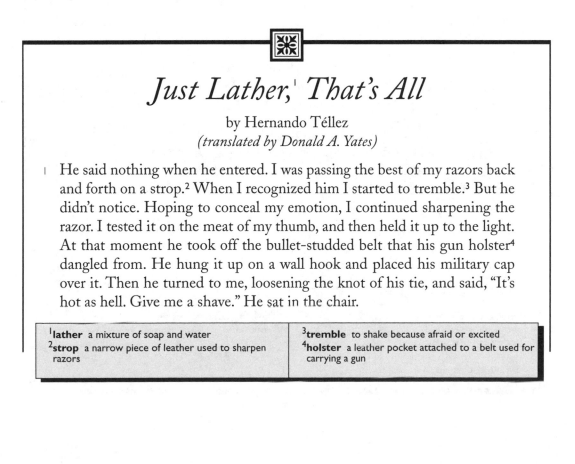

Just Lather,[1] That's All

by Hernando Téllez
(translated by Donald A. Yates)

He said nothing when he entered. I was passing the best of my razors back and forth on a strop.[2] When I recognized him I started to tremble.[3] But he didn't notice. Hoping to conceal my emotion, I continued sharpening the razor. I tested it on the meat of my thumb, and then held it up to the light. At that moment he took off the bullet-studded belt that his gun holster[4] dangled from. He hung it up on a wall hook and placed his military cap over it. Then he turned to me, loosening the knot of his tie, and said, "It's hot as hell. Give me a shave." He sat in the chair.

---

[1] **lather** a mixture of soap and water
[2] **strop** a narrow piece of leather used to sharpen razors

[3] **tremble** to shake because afraid or excited
[4] **holster** a leather pocket attached to a belt used for carrying a gun

2   I estimated he had a four-day beard. The four days taken up by the latest expedition in search of our troops.[5] His face reddened, burned by the sun. Carefully, I began to prepare the soap. I cut off a few slices, dropped them into the cup, mixed in a bit of warm water, and began to stir with a brush. Immediately the foam began to rise. "The other boys in the group should have this much beard, too." I continued stirring the lather.

3   "But we did all right, you know. We got the main ones. We brought back some dead, and we've got some others still alive. But pretty soon they'll all be dead."

4   "How many did you catch," I asked.

5   "Fourteen. We had to go plenty deep into the woods to find them. But we'll get even.[6] Not one of them comes out of this alive, not one." He leaned back on the chair when he saw me with the lathered brush in my hand. I still had to put the sheet on him. No doubt about it, I was upset. I took a sheet out of the drawer and knotted[7] it around my customer's neck. He wouldn't stop talking. He probably thought I was in sympathy with[8] his party.

6   "The town must have learned a lesson from what we did the other day,"[9] he said.

7   "Yes," I replied, securing the knot at his dark, sweaty neck.

8   "That was a fine show, eh?"

Make predictions: *What will the customer tell the barber about what they did the other day? What "lesson" is he referring to? How will the barber react?*

9   "Very good," I answered, turning back for the brush. The man closed his eyes with a gesture of fatigue[10] and sat waiting for the cool caress of the soap. I had never had him so close to me. The day he ordered the whole town to file into the patio of the school to see the four rebels hanging there, I came face-to-face with him for an instant. But the sight of the mutilated[11] bodies kept[12] me from noticing the face of a man who had directed it all, the face I was now about to take into my own hands. It was not an unpleasant face, certainly. And the beard, which made him seem a bit older than he was, didn't suit him badly at all. His name was Torres.

---

[5]**troops** soldiers
[6]**get even** get revenge
[7]**knotted** tied together
[8]**in sympathy with** supportive of
[9]**the other day** within the last few days

[10]**fatigue** extreme tiredness
[11]**mutilated** violently damaged, especially by cutting off pieces
[12]**kept** stopped

Captain Torres. A man of imagination, because who else would have thought of hanging the naked rebels and then holding target practice on certain parts of their bodies? I began to apply the first layer of soap. With his eyes closed, he continued. "Without any effort I could go straight to sleep," he said, "but there's plenty to do this afternoon." I stopped the lathering and asked with a feigned[13] look of interest: "A firing squad?"[14] "Something like that, but a little slower." I got on with the job of lathering his beard. My hands started trembling again. The man could not possibly realize it, and this was in my favor.[15] But I would have preferred that he hadn't come. It was likely that many of our faction had seen him enter. And an enemy soldier under one's roof imposes[16] certain conditions. I would be obliged to shave that beard like any other one, carefully, gently, like that of any customer, taking pains to see that no single pore emitted[17] a drop of blood. Being careful to see that the little tufts of hair did not lead the blade astray.[18] Seeing that his skin ended up clean, soft, and healthy, so that passing the back of my hand over it I couldn't feel a hair. Yes, I was secretly a rebel, but I was also a conscientious barber, and proud of the preciseness[19] of my profession. And this four days' growth of beard was a fitting challenge.

10   I took the razor, opened up the two protective arms, exposed the blade and began the job, from one of the sideburns[20] downward. The razor responded beautifully. His beard was inflexible and hard, not too long, but thick. Bit by bit the skin emerged.[21] The razor rasped along, making its customary sound as fluffs of lather mixed with bits of hair gathered along the blade. I paused a moment to clean it, then took up the strop again to sharpen the razor, because I'm a barber who does things properly. The man, who had kept his eyes closed, opened them now, removed one of his hands from under the sheet, felt the spot on his face where the soap had been cleared off, and said, "Come to the school today at six o'clock." "The same thing as the other day?" I asked, horrified. "It could be better," he replied. "What do you plan to do?" "I don't know yet. But we'll amuse ourselves." Once more he leaned back and closed his eyes. I approached him with the razor poised. "Do you plan to punish them all?" I ventured timidly. "All." The soap was drying on his face. I had to hurry. In the mirror I looked toward the street. It was the same as ever: the grocery store with two or three customers in it. Then I glanced at the clock: two twenty in the afternoon. The razor continued on its downward stroke. Now from

---

[13]**feigned** pretended

[14]**firing squad** a group of soldiers who shoot and kill prisoners

[15]**in my favor** to my advantage

[16]**impose** to make necessary

[17]**emitted** gave out, produced

[18]**lead the blade astray** make the blade go the wrong way

[19]**preciseness** exactness

[20]**sideburns** hair on the sides of a man's face, in front of the ears

[21]**emerged** appeared after being hidden

the other sideburn down. A thick, blue beard. He should have let it grow like some poets or priests do. It would suit him well. A lot of people wouldn't recognize him. Much to his benefit, I thought, as I attempted to cover the neck area smoothly. There, for sure, the razor had to be handled masterfully, since the hair, although softer, grew into little swirls. A curly beard. One of the tiny pores could be opened up and issue forth its pearl of blood. A good barber such as I prides himself in never allowing this to happen to a client. And this was a first-class client. How many of us had he ordered shot? How many of us had he ordered mutilated? It was better not to think about it. Torres did not know that I was his enemy. He did not know it nor did the rest. It was a secret shared by very few, precisely so that I could inform the revolutionaries of what Torres was doing in the town and of what he was planning each time he undertook a rebel-hunting excursion. So it was going to be very difficult to explain that I had him right in my hands and let him go peacefully—alive and shaved.

Make predictions: What is the barber's dilemma? What will he do about it?

The beard was now almost completely gone. He seemed younger, less burdened by years than when he had arrived. I suppose this always happens with men who visit barbershops. Under one stroke of my razor Torres was being rejuvenated[22]—rejuvenated because I am a good barber, the best in the town, if I may say so. A little more lather here, under his chin, on his Adam's apple, on this big vein. How hot it is getting! Torres must be sweating as much as I. But he is not afraid. He is a calm man, who is not even thinking about what he is going to do with the prisoners this afternoon. On the other hand I, with this razor in my hands, stroking and restroking this skin, trying to keep blood from oozing from these pores, can't even think clearly. Damn him for coming, because I am a revolutionary and not a murderer. And how easy it would be to kill him. And he deserves it. Does he? No! What the devil! No one deserves to have someone else make the sacrifice of becoming a murderer. What do you gain by it? Nothing. Others come along and still others, and the first ones kill the second ones and they the next ones and it goes on like this until everything is a sea of blood. I could cut his throat just so, zip! zip! I wouldn't give him time to complain and since he has his eyes closed he wouldn't see the glistening knife blade or my glistening eyes. But I'm trembling like a real murderer. Out of his neck a gush of blood would spout

---

[22]**rejuvenated** made to look or feel younger

onto the sheet, on the chair, on my hands, on the floor. I would have to close the door. And the blood would keep inching along the floor, warm, ineradicable,[23] uncontainable, until it reached the street, like a little scarlet stream. I'm sure that one solid stroke, one deep incision,[24] would prevent any pain. He wouldn't suffer. But what would I do with the body? Where would I hide it? I would have to flee,[25] leaving all I have behind, and take refuge[26] far away, far, far away. But they would follow until they found me. "Captain Torres' murderer. He slit his throat while he was shaving him—a coward." And then on the other side. "The avenger[27] of us all. A name to remember. (And here they would mention my name.) He was a town barber. No one knew he was defending[28] our cause."[29]

12   And what of all this? Murderer or hero? My destiny depends on the edge of this blade. I can turn my hand a bit more, press a little harder on the razor, and sink it in. The skin would give way like silk, like rubber, like the strop. There is nothing more tender than human skin and the blood is always there, ready to pour forth. A blade like this doesn't fail. It is my best. But I don't want to be a murderer, no sir. You came to me for a shave. And I perform my work honorably . . . . I don't want blood on my hands. Just lather, that's all. You are an executioner and I am only a barber. Each person has his own place in the scheme of things. That's right. His own place.

Make predictions: What will the barber do? What will the customer do? How will the story end?

13   Now his chin had been stroked clean and smooth. The man sat up and looked into the mirror. He rubbed his hands over his skin and felt it fresh, like new.

14   "Thanks," he said. He went to the hanger for his belt, pistol and cap. I must have been very pale; my shirt felt soaked. Torres finished adjusting the buckle, straightened his pistol in the holster and after automatically smoothing down his hair, he put on the cap. From his pants pocket he took out several coins to pay me for my services. And he began to head toward the door. In the doorway he paused for a moment, and turning to me he said:

15   "They told me that you'd kill me. I came to find out. But killing isn't easy. You can take my word for it."[30] And he headed on down the street.

---

[23]**ineradicable** impossible to remove, permanent
[24]**incision** cut
[25]**flee** to run away, to escape
[26]**take refuge** to hide from danger

[27]**avenger** someone who seeks or gets revenge
[28]**defending** supporting, protecting
[29]**cause** a belief or goal shared by a group of people
[30]**take my word for it** believe me

THINKING ABOUT THE STORY

Comprehension

Discuss the following questions as a class.

1. Who are the two characters? Describe them.
2. What does the barber do when he recognizes the customer? Why?
3. What does the customer tell the barber about the latest expedition? How does the barber react?
4. What does the customer imply that he will do that afternoon? How does the barber react?
5. How does the barber feel about his job? How does he describe the way he does his work?
6. Why doesn't the barber kill the customer?
7. What happens at the end of the story? Does this ending surprise you? Explain.

Focus on Literature: Conflict

Conflict is a struggle between two opposing people or forces. Conflict can be *internal* or *external*. An *internal conflict* takes place in the mind of a character. For example, a character may struggle with his or her fear of doing something. An *external conflict* can be between characters (for example, a struggle between a father and son) or between a character and nature (for example, a struggle between firefighters and a fire). In fiction, one or more types of conflict may be present.

Discuss the following questions as a class.

1. Describe the conflict or conflicts in "Just Lather, That's All." Who or what are the opposing people and forces?
2. Is the conflict in the story internal, external, or both? Explain.
3. Through whose point of view do we see the conflict? Why do you think the author chose this point of view?
4. How does the title "Just Lather, That's All" relate to the conflict in the story? Why do you think the author chose this title?

Expansion

Discuss the following questions in small groups.

1. If you were the captain, would you have gone to the barber for a shave? Explain.
2. If you were the barber, would you have killed the captain? Explain.
3. As you learned in Unit 5, characters can be round or flat, sympathetic or unsympathetic. Describe the characters. Are they round or flat? Sympathetic or unsympathetic? Explain.
4. Do you think a person, government, or other group ever has the right to kill someone? Explain.
5. Describe a conflict you have faced. How did you resolve it?

Responding to the Story

Write about one of the following topics.

1. **What Would You Have Done?** Imagine that you were the barber in the story "Just Lather, That's All." What would you have done? Write a paragraph or essay explaining whether you agree or disagree with the barber's actions and his reasons. Explain whether you would have acted differently. If so, what would you have done? Why?

2. **Facing a Conflict.** Write about a time when you faced a conflict. Describe the conflict and how you resolved it.

3. **Capital Punishment.** *Capital punishment* is the legal right to kill someone who has been found guilty of committing a serious crime. Do you think a government or other group ever has the right to kill someone? If so, explain why, for which crimes, and with which method of execution. If not, explain why not, and what alternative punishment should be used for serious crimes.

Peer Response

Work with a partner. Exchange papers and read each other's writing. Discuss the following questions.

- Does the writer describe a conflict? If so, what is it?
- Does anything surprise you? If so, what surprises you?
- Is the writer convincing? Explain.
- Do you have any questions for the writer?
- What do you like best about the writing?

After you discuss your ideas, you may want to revise your writing.

About the Author

Hernando Téllez (1908–1966) was born and educated in Bogotá, Colombia. He worked as a journalist for some of Colombia's most popular newspapers and magazines. His short story collection, *Cenizas al viento* (Ashes in the wind), made him internationally famous.

Nearing 90

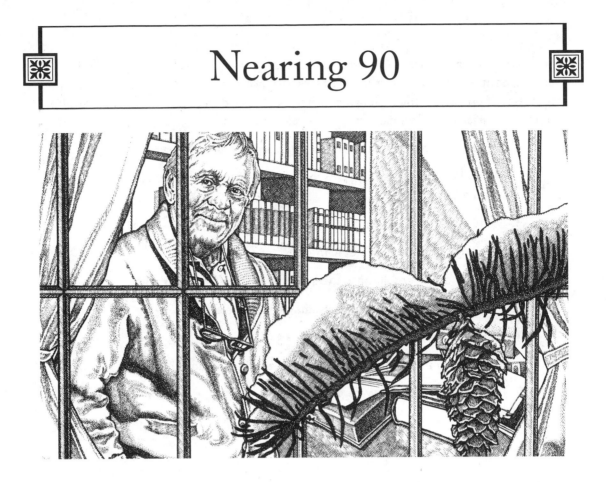

SETTING THE CONTEXT

Discussion

Discuss the following questions as a class.

1. Do you like being your present age? Would you prefer to be a different age? Explain.
2. How do people generally view age in your country? Do they think it is better to be young or old? Explain.
3. Why do some young people want to be older?
4. Why do some old people want to be younger?

Vocabulary

The boldfaced words in the following sentences are from the essay on pages 183–185. Use the context to guess the meanings of the boldfaced words. Use a dictionary if necessary. Then match the boldfaced words with the correct definitions that follow. Compare your answers in small groups.

_____ 1. The owners didn't take care of the house, so it **deteriorated** badly.

_____ 2. When he stopped reading newspapers, Frank **lost touch with** the international news.

_____ 3. Stand up straight! It's important to have good **posture**.

_____ 4. All living things die; it's **inevitable**.

_____ 5. Without an air conditioner, the summer heat was **unbearable**.

_____ 6. If we don't protect rare animals, they will face **extinction**.

_____ 7. Too much salt **spoils** the soup.

_____ 8. Your essay has two **flaws**. The main idea isn't clear and the support is weak.

_____ 9. Most people have a few **regrets** about some choices they have made.

_____ 10. Lynne is not very **materialistic**; she lives simply and has few possessions.

a. ruins, destroys
b. death
c. problems
d. interested in getting money and things
e. very painful or unpleasant
f. didn't know anymore, forgot about
g. became worse
h. certain to happen
i. how you hold your body when sitting or standing
j. sadness about having done or not having done something

READING THE ESSAY

As you read the essay, think about the title. Why do you think the author wrote this essay? Why is nearing ninety important to him?

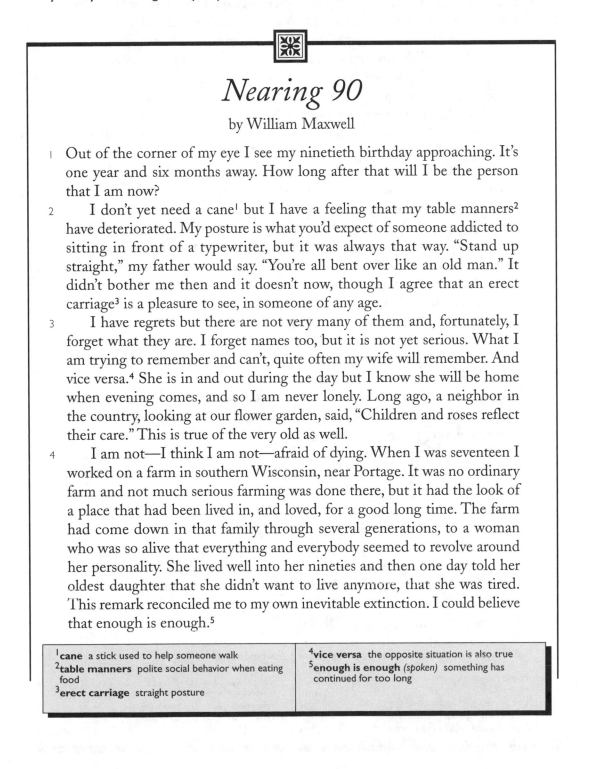

Nearing 90

by William Maxwell

1   Out of the corner of my eye I see my ninetieth birthday approaching. It's one year and six months away. How long after that will I be the person that I am now?

2   I don't yet need a cane[1] but I have a feeling that my table manners[2] have deteriorated. My posture is what you'd expect of someone addicted to sitting in front of a typewriter, but it was always that way. "Stand up straight," my father would say. "You're all bent over like an old man." It didn't bother me then and it doesn't now, though I agree that an erect carriage[3] is a pleasure to see, in someone of any age.

3   I have regrets but there are not very many of them and, fortunately, I forget what they are. I forget names too, but it is not yet serious. What I am trying to remember and can't, quite often my wife will remember. And vice versa.[4] She is in and out during the day but I know she will be home when evening comes, and so I am never lonely. Long ago, a neighbor in the country, looking at our flower garden, said, "Children and roses reflect their care." This is true of the very old as well.

4   I am not—I think I am not—afraid of dying. When I was seventeen I worked on a farm in southern Wisconsin, near Portage. It was no ordinary farm and not much serious farming was done there, but it had the look of a place that had been lived in, and loved, for a good long time. The farm had come down in that family through several generations, to a woman who was so alive that everything and everybody seemed to revolve around her personality. She lived well into her nineties and then one day told her oldest daughter that she didn't want to live anymore, that she was tired. This remark reconciled me to my own inevitable extinction. I could believe that enough is enough.[5]

[1]**cane** a stick used to help someone walk
[2]**table manners** polite social behavior when eating food
[3]**erect carriage** straight posture

[4]**vice versa** the opposite situation is also true
[5]**enough is enough** (*spoken*) something has continued for too long

5   Because I actively enjoy sleeping, dreams, the unexplainable dialogues that take place in my head as I am drifting off, all that, I tell myself that lying down to an afternoon nap that goes on and on through eternity is not something to be concerned about. What spoils this pleasant fancy is the recollection that when people are dead they don't read books. This I find unbearable. No Tolstoy, no Chekhov, no Elizabeth Bowen, no Keats, no Rilke. One might as well be—

6   Before I am ready to call it quits[6] I would like to reread every book I have ever deeply enjoyed, beginning with Jane Austen and going through shelf after shelf of the bookcases, until I arrive at the "Autobiographies" of William Butler Yeats. As it is, I read a great deal of the time. I am harder to please, though. I see flaws in masterpieces. Conrad indulging in rhetoric[7] when he would do better to get on with it.[8] I would read all day long and well into the night if there were no other claims on[9] my time. Appointments with doctors, with the dentist. The monthly bank statement. Income tax returns. And because I don't want to turn into a monster, people. Afternoon tea with X, dinner with the Ys. Our social life would be a good deal more active than it is if more than half of those I care about hadn't passed over to the other side.[10]

7   I did not wholly escape that amnesia[11] that overtakes[12] children around the age of six but I carried along with me more of my childhood than, I think, most people do. Once, after dinner, my father hitched up the horse and took my mother and me for a sleigh[13] ride. The winter stars were very bright. The sleigh bells made a lovely sound. I was bundled up to the nose, between my father and mother, where nothing, not even the cold, could get at me. The very perfection of happiness.

8   At something like the same age, I went for a ride, again with my father and mother, on a riverboat at Havana, Illinois. It was a side-wheeler and the decks were screened,[14] I suppose as a protection against mosquitoes. Across eight decades the name of the steamboat comes back to me—the *Eastland*—bringing with it the context of disaster. A year later, at the dock in Chicago, too many of the passengers crowded on one side, waving good-bye, and it rolled over and sank.[15] Trapped by the screens everywhere, a great many people lost their lives. The fact that I had been on this very steamboat, that I had escaped from a watery grave, I continued to remember all through my childhood.

---

[6]**call it quits** to stop doing something you have done for a long time

[7]**rhetoric** writing that sounds important but isn't very useful

[8]**get on with it** to continue doing what's important

[9]**claims on** requests or demands for

[10]**passed over to the other side** died

[11]**amnesia** loss of memory

[12]**overtake** to suddenly affect

[13]**sleigh** a large vehicle pulled by a horse used for traveling on snow

[14]**screened** protected by a wire net

[15]**sank** went down below the water's surface

9   I have liked remembering almost as much as I have liked living. But now it is different. I have to be careful. I can ruin a night's sleep by suddenly, in the dark, thinking about some particular time in my life. Before I can stop myself it is as if I had driven a mine shaft down through layers and layers of the past and must explore, relive, remember, reconsider, until daylight delivers me.

10   I have not forgotten the pleasure, when our children were very young, of hoisting them onto my shoulders when their legs gave out. Of reading to them at bedtime. Of studying their beautiful faces. But that was more than thirty years ago. I admire the way that, as adults, they have taken hold of[16] life, and I am glad that they are not materialistic, but there is little or nothing I can do for them at this point,[17] except write a little fable to put in their Christmas stocking.[18]

11   "Are you writing?" people ask—out of politeness, undoubtedly. And I say, "Nothing very much." The truth but not the whole truth—which is that I seem to have lost touch with the place that stories and novels come from. I have no idea why. I still like making sentences.

12   Every now and then, in my waking moments, and especially when I am in the country, I stand and look hard at everything.

[16]**taken hold of** taken responsibility for [17]**at this point** now	[18]**Christmas stocking** a long sock hung by the fireplace at Christmas that is filled with small gifts for children

THINKING ABOUT THE ESSAY

Comprehension

Discuss the following questions as a class.

1. How old was the author when he wrote this essay?
2. What does he want to do before he dies?
3. Why does he say that he's not afraid of dying?
4. What events from his childhood does he remember? Why do you think he remembers them?
5. What events does he remember from when his children were young? Why do you think he remembers them?
6. Reread paragraph 12. Why do you think the author ends his essay in this way? Explain.

Focus on Reading: Phrasal Verbs

Like an idiom, a *phrasal verb* is an expression that has a different meaning from its individual words. A phrasal verb is a combination of a verb and adverb and/or preposition. Often you can guess the meaning of a phrasal verb from the words around it. Look at this example from paragraph 8 of "Nearing 90":

A year later, at the dock in Chicago, too many passengers crowded on one side, waving good-bye, and [the boat] **rolled over** *and sank.*

The context gives the clues that the phrasal verb *roll over* means to move forward and down, in a circular way.

The boldfaced phrasal verbs in the following sentences are from the essay. Use the context to guess their meanings. Use a dictionary if necessary. Then match them with the correct definitions that follow.

_____ 1. Last winter, we really **bundled up** to keep warm.

_____ 2. Jeff **is addicted to** eating chocolate; he eats it whenever he can.

_____ 3. If she works hard, Alice will **turn into** a great artist.

_____ 4. When children **indulge in** eating too much candy, they can get sick.

_____ 5. Martha's life **revolves around** her family and friends. She is always doing something with them or for them.

_____ 6. If you **look hard at** the painting, you'll appreciate all the details.

_____ 7. I did not sleep well last night, so I was **drifting off** in class this afternoon.

_____ 8. After I broke my leg, I **reconciled** myself **to** a period of inactivity.

_____ 9. How are you **getting on with** your writing project? Will you finish it on time?

_____ 10. We **hitched up** the trailer to the car and moved to our new house.

a. prepared to accept something unpleasant
b. become
c. observe or watch carefully
d. dressed in a lot of warm clothing
e. allow oneself to enjoy something, even if it's not healthy
f. attached or fastened
g. making progress with something, such as a job
h. centers or focuses on
i. is unable to stop doing something
j. falling asleep

Focus on Literature: Flashbacks

Sometimes writers present scenes that happened before the time the story occurs. These scenes, called *flashbacks*, give the reader helpful background information about a character, place, or event. Writers create flashbacks by using memories, dreams, and personal stories. Since flashbacks refer to the past, writers often introduce them with time words or expressions, such as *when*, *long ago*, and *once*.

Discuss the following questions in small groups.

1. Underline the flashback in Paragraph 2. How does it relate to what the author is writing about?
2. Underline the flashback in Paragraph 3. What three things does the author compare?
3. Underline the flashback in Paragraph 4. Why do you think the author includes this memory?
4. What memory does the author describe in Paragraph 7? What background information does this give you?
5. What two events does the author recall in Paragraph 8? How are they related?
6. Underline the flashback in Paragraph 10. What background information does this give you? How is it related to the author now?

Expansion

Discuss the following questions in small groups.

1. The author describes some events that he remembers clearly from his childhood. What events from your childhood do you remember most clearly?
2. The author says that he doesn't have many regrets. Do you have any regrets? If so, what are they?
3. The author accomplished many things in his life. What accomplishments are you most proud of?
4. Are you looking forward to your next birthday? Explain.

RESPONDING TO THE ESSAY

Write about one the following topics.

1. **Nearing . . . .** William Maxwell wrote an essay about his approaching ninetieth birthday. Write about an approaching birthday. Use the following questions to help you.

   • How old will you be?
   • How do you feel about becoming this age?
   • What is special to you about this age?
   • Do you have any regrets? If so, what are they?

2. **Accomplishments.** William Maxwell accomplished many things in his life. Write one paragraph about your accomplishments and one paragraph about what you want to accomplish. Use the following steps to help you.

   • List the accomplishments that you are most proud of.
   • List things that you really want to accomplish.
   • Write a paragraph about your accomplishments. Explain why you are proud of them.
   • Write a paragraph about things that you really want to accomplish. Explain why they are important and how you plan to accomplish them.

3. **A Favorite Memory.** William Maxwell recalls a childhood memory that was the "very perfection of happiness." Write about a happy childhood memory. Use the following questions to help you.

   • How old were you?
   • Where were you?
   • Who were you with?
   • What were you doing?

   Add sensory images to help your readers experience your memory.

Peer Response

Work with a partner. Exchange papers and read each other's writing. Discuss the following questions.

- Does the writer use any phrasal verbs?
- Does the writer use any flashbacks? If so, what background information did you learn?
- What did you learn about the writer?
- Do you have any questions for the writer?
- What do you like best about the writing?

After you discuss your ideas, you may want to revise your writing.

About the Author

William Maxwell was born in Lincoln, Illinois, in 1908. After receiving a B.A. from the University of Illinois and an M.A. from Harvard University, he taught English at the University of Illinois. Then he worked at *The New Yorker* magazine from 1936 to 1976, first in the art department and then as a fiction editor. William Maxwell's books include *Bright Center of Heaven*, *They Came Like Swallows*, and *All the Days and Nights*. He won the National Book Award, the PEN/Malamud Award, and the Howells Medal of the American Academy of Arts and Letters. "Nearing 90" is from the anthology *In Brief: Short Takes on the Personal*. William Maxwell died in 2000.

Immortality

SETTING THE CONTEXT

Discussion

Discuss the following questions as a class.

1. What are the people in the picture doing? How old do you think they are? How do you think they feel?
2. Would this activity happen in your country? Explain.
3. Young people sometimes feel like they are immortal, like they will live forever. Why do you think they feel this way?
4. How might feeling immortal influence a person's behavior? Explain.

Vocabulary

The boldfaced words in the following sentences are from the story on pages 192–193. Use the context to guess the meanings of the boldfaced words. Use a dictionary if necessary. Then match the boldfaced words with the correct definitions that follow. Compare your answers in small groups.

_____ 1. She was late for work because she **got stuck** in traffic.

_____ 2. Lloyd is **beating** Bruce in the race, but Bruce could still win.

_____ 3. The man **swore** loudly when he dropped the heavy box on his foot.

_____ 4. I've never **had the nerve** to go skiing. It looks so dangerous!

_____ 5. My brother **has the brains** to do well in school, but he doesn't like to study.

_____ 6. When a dog ran in front of my car, I had to **swerve** to avoid hitting it.

_____ 7. I just cleaned my room, so please don't **mess** it **up**.

_____ 8. We had a really **tough** math test today. I hope I passed it.

a. turn suddenly and dangerously
b. was unable to move
c. difficult
d. defeating, doing better than
e. is intelligent
f. been brave enough
g. make untidy
h. used bad language

READING THE STORY

As you read the story, think about the title. How does it relate to the story?

Immortality

by Maria Testa

1   I was only fourteen at the time and couldn't drive, otherwise I would have been at the wheel,[1] I was sure of it. My mother always said that I had more nerve than brains, and everyone knew I had a lot of brains. My sister, Sandra, who was driving, still remembers how I put my hand on that cop's[2] gun while he was wearing it in his holster. I just put my hand on it, and he put his hand on top of mine. I wasn't even scared, though Sandra, who was thirteen then, almost died. You don't mess with[3] cops, she still says. But I just smiled up at him, and he took his hand off mine and put it on top of my head like he was going to mess up my hair. I let him keep it there for a couple of seconds before I ducked away.[4] It wasn't like I cared about my hair or anything. It's thick and black and tough to mess up.

2   But even my hair was really messed up that night in Sandra's car. We had all the windows open, and Sandra was driving so fast that I wouldn't have been surprised if my hair blew right off. Sandra's friend Laura was screaming her head off[5] in the backseat, but I knew she was loving it because we were winning. We were beating the guys. Mikey and Tony were gaining on us[6] over in the left lane,[7] but they were stuck. They'd never make the exit from there.

3   It was time for us to cut over, and as I slapped both hands against the dashboard,[8] Sandra swore in Italian and swerved neatly across two lanes. The guys shot past[9] us on the left as the Gano Street sign disappeared over our heads. Then we heard the sirens.[10] We had been speeding our brains out[11] all the way from Newport[12] since I had suggested we make a race out of the ride back to Providence,[13] and it was some kind of miracle that we hadn't seen any cops the whole way. Until now. The cops whipped past[14] us as we slowed down heading toward the exit ramp.[15] They were chasing Mikey and Tony, and I hoped those guys knew enough to let themselves get caught.

---

[1] **at the wheel** driving
[2] **cop** *(informal)* a police officer
[3] **mess with** to annoy or argue with
[4] **ducked away** moved one's body or head away
[5] **screaming her head off** screaming very loudly
[6] **gaining on us** getting closer to us
[7] **lane** part of a road, often divided by painted lines
[8] **dashboard** the control board at the front of a car

[9] **shot past** went by very fast
[10] **sirens** loud warning sounds
[11] **speeding our brains out** *(informal)* driving very fast
[12] **Newport** city in Rhode Island
[13] **Providence** capital city of Rhode Island
[14] **whipped past** went by very fast
[15] **exit ramp** road for driving off a main road

4   The race was over. The China Inn was less than ten minutes away doing the speed limit.[16] It would have been a lot more fun to screech[17] into the parking lot, neck and neck[18] with the guys, but I knew they'd make it eventually, with a lot to say. I thought about General Tsao's chicken and broccoli and rice . . . and Mikey snuggling up[19] next to Sandra, but saving a wink[20] for me.

5   We decided to hang out[21] in the parking lot and wait. My cousin, Tina, climbed out of the backseat and slammed the door. I had almost forgotten she was with us, with all the wind blowing and Laura screaming and sirens wailing. She didn't say a word but stared straight at me, her eyes looking like two big black olives, the kind with the pits already out.

6   Why did she have to look at me like that when she knew I was the youngest and not responsible? Everyone else was at least two years older than me, and no one was stupid. I think, at that moment, I hated her, but even then I didn't really know why. She wasn't the only one with big, dark eyes. And she wasn't the only one thinking about death.

[16]**doing the speed limit** driving at the fastest speed allowed by law
[17]**screech** to make a high, loud sound, as when a car starts or stops suddenly
[18]**neck and neck** (informal) with an equal chance of winning a race
[19]**snuggling up** sitting very close
[20]**wink** closing and opening one eye quickly to show amusement
[21]**hang out** (informal) spend time

THINKING ABOUT THE STORY

Comprehension

Discuss the following questions as a class.

1. How old was the narrator in the story?
2. Was the narrator older or younger than the others in the car?
3. Who was driving the car? About how old was she?
4. What were the girls doing? Whose idea was it?
5. Who was in the other car? How do you think they know the girls?
6. Which car did the police chase? Why do you think they chased it?
7. Where did the girls wait for the boys? What did they plan to do there?
8. How do you think Tina felt about the race? Explain.
9. Why was Tina staring at the narrator?

Focus on Literature: Mood

Mood is the feeling a writer tries to create for the reader. The mood can be happy, sad, excited, angry, or another feeling. Writers use powerful words and images to create the story's mood. For example, Lensey Namioka uses humorous images, situations, and characters to create a comical mood in "The All-American Slurp" in Unit 1. In contrast, Hernando Téllez uses serious events, opposing characters, and violent images to create a suspenseful mood in "Just Lather, That's All" in this unit.

Make a word map with your feelings about the story.

1. How did you feel as you read the story? Write an adjective describing your mood in the middle circle.

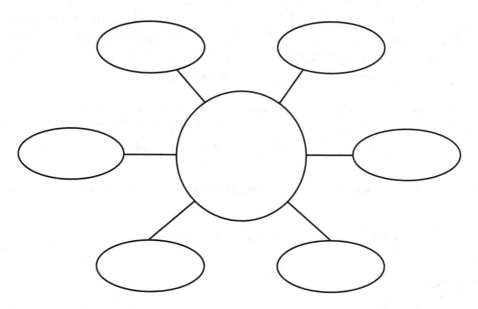

2. Reread the story. Underline the words and images that help create this mood. Then write these words and images in the surrounding circles.
3. Compare and discuss your word maps in small groups.

Focus on Reading: Register

Register is the level of formality people use when they talk or write to each other. It includes vocabulary, style, and grammar. People's choice of register usually depends on who they're talking or writing to. Generally, they talk and write more informally to people who are of similar age and status. For example, young people talking to their friends usually use colloquial and slang vocabulary, an informal style, and imperfect grammar. However, when talking to adults they often use standard vocabulary, a more formal style, and better grammar. Writers try to choose appropriate registers for their characters so their speech sounds natural. They also use register to show relationships among characters.

Discuss the following questions as a class.

1. Describe the narrator's register. Is it formal or informal? How do you know?
2. Why do you think she uses this register?
3. How do you express formal or informal registers in your native language? Do you choose different vocabulary? Style? Grammar? Give examples.

Expansion

Discuss the following questions in small groups.

1. How do you think the characters felt at the end of the story? Do you think the car race changed them? If so, how?
2. The narrator's mother always said that she had "more nerve than brains." Do you know anyone who fits this description? If so, describe him or her.
3. Do you identify with (or feel sympathetic toward) any character in the story? If so, which one? Why?
4. Have you ever done something dangerous with your friends? If so, describe the experience. Would you do the same thing now? Why or why not?

Responding to the Story

Write about one of the following topics.

1. **Living Dangerously.** Have you (or has anyone you know) ever done something dangerous? If so, write a paragraph about it. Describe the experience and the mood. Explain how you feel about the experience now.

2. **Retelling the Story.** Imagine that the narrator of "Immortality" has to write a report about the car race for a police officer. How would her use of language be different? Retell the story, using standard vocabulary, a formal style, and correct grammar.

3. **Another Point of View.** "Immortality" is told from the narrator's point of view. Try to imagine what the other characters (for example, the narrator's sister, Tina, Mikey, or a police officer) think and feel about the event. Retell the story from another character's point of view.

Peer Response

Work with a partner. Exchange papers and read each other's writing. Discuss the following questions.

- Who narrates the story?
- Describe the register. Is it formal or informal?
- Does the writing create a special mood? If so, describe it.
- Do you have any questions for the writer?
- What do you like best about the writing?

After you discuss your ideas, you may want to revise your writing.

About the Author

Maria Testa is a writer and a lawyer. She has written short stories for several magazines. "Immortality" is from her collection of stories called *Dancing Pink Flamingos*.

The Delight Song of Tsoai-Talee

SETTING THE CONTEXT

Discussion

1. *Delight* is a feeling of great pleasure, wonder, or joy. What gives you delight? Brainstorm ideas, images, and feelings that give you delight. Complete the following word map with the ideas, images, and feelings you brainstormed.

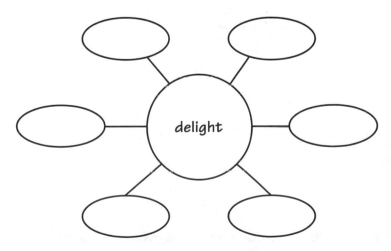

2. Compare your word maps in small groups. Which ideas, images, and feelings are similar? Which are different?

3. If you like, add some of your classmates' ideas, images, and feelings to your map.

READING THE POEM

The poet, N. Scott Momaday, is a member of the Kiowa nation. The Kiowa lived on the southern plains of the United States, before being forced onto reservations in the middle and late nineteenth century. Like many Native Americans, the Kiowa have used storytelling to pass on their traditions for hundreds of years. Native Americans consider words very powerful—so powerful, in fact, that they can create and shape the world. As you read the poem, think about the power of the words and images. Why do you think the poet uses these words? What does he value most in life? What is his relationship to these things?

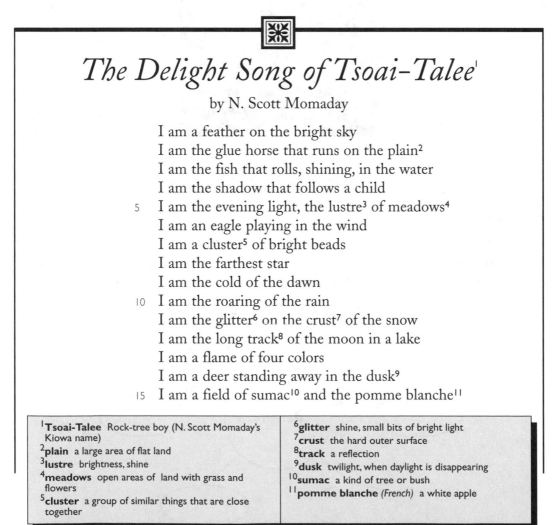

The Delight Song of Tsoai-Talee[1]

by N. Scott Momaday

I am a feather on the bright sky
I am the glue horse that runs on the plain[2]
I am the fish that rolls, shining, in the water
I am the shadow that follows a child
5   I am the evening light, the lustre[3] of meadows[4]
I am an eagle playing in the wind
I am a cluster[5] of bright beads
I am the farthest star
I am the cold of the dawn
10   I am the roaring of the rain
I am the glitter[6] on the crust[7] of the snow
I am the long track[8] of the moon in a lake
I am a flame of four colors
I am a deer standing away in the dusk[9]
15   I am a field of sumac[10] and the pomme blanche[11]

[1]**Tsoai-Talee** Rock-tree boy (N. Scott Momaday's Kiowa name)
[2]**plain** a large area of flat land
[3]**lustre** brightness, shine
[4]**meadows** open areas of land with grass and flowers
[5]**cluster** a group of similar things that are close together

[6]**glitter** shine, small bits of bright light
[7]**crust** the hard outer surface
[8]**track** a reflection
[9]**dusk** twilight, when daylight is disappearing
[10]**sumac** a kind of tree or bush
[11]**pomme blanche** (French) a white apple

I am an angle of geese in the winter sky
I am the hunger of a young wolf
I am the whole dream of these things

You see, I am alive, I am alive
20   I stand in good relation[12] to the earth
I stand in good relation to the gods
I stand in good relation to all that is beautiful
I stand in good relation to the daughter of *Tsen-tainte*[13]
You see, I am alive, I am alive

[12]**in good relation to** in harmony with   [13]**Tsen-tainte** White Horse

THINKING ABOUT THE POEM

Comprehension

Discuss the following questions as a class.

1. The poem has two parts. Which part has a narrower, more specific focus? Which part has a broader, more general focus?
2. What subject pronoun does the poet use in the first part? Who do you think he is talking to?
3. What additional subject pronoun does he use in the second part? Who do you think he is talking to?
4. What verbs does the poet repeat in the poem? Why do you think he repeats them?

Focus on Literature: List Poem

> A list poem consists of a list of items that are similar or related in some way and have special meaning to the poet. The items in the list can be people, places, things, events, experiences, or ideas.

Discuss the following questions as a class.

1. What kinds of items are listed in the poem?
2. How are the listed items similar or related to each other?
3. Why do you think these items have special meaning to the poet?

Focus on Literature: Chant

> The *chant* is one of the oldest forms of poetry. It has an open, spontaneous form, and it does not require a specific beginning, middle, or end. In a chant, one or more lines are repeated again and again. This repetition is a powerful force; it adds energy and strength to a poem. Repetition also creates rhythm—a kind of musical pattern—so chants are similar to a song. Poets and songwriters often use repetition to add force to a main idea or theme.

"The Delight Song of Tsoai-Talee" is a chant that celebrates life. Reread the poem aloud. Listen to the repetition and rhythm. Then discuss the following questions in small groups.

1. What words or phrases does the poet repeat in the first part of the poem?
2. What words or phrases does the poet repeat in the second part?
3. Do you think the use of repetition adds power to the poem? Explain.
4. What main idea or theme do you think the poet is trying to express?
5. Does his use of repetition add emphasis to the main idea or theme? Explain.

Expansion

A. The poem contains images related to the four basic elements: earth, air, fire, and water. Complete the following chart with images from the poem that describe each element. Then compare your answers in small groups.

Earth	Air	Fire	Water
horse on the plain			

B. Discuss the following questions as a class.

1. Describe your feelings as you read this poem. What images helped create these feelings?
2. The images describe the poet's feelings toward the subject of his poem. How do you think he feels about this subject?
3. The poet mentions Tsoai-Talee and the daughter of Tsen-tainte in this poem. Why do you think he mentions them?

Responding to the Poem

Write about one of the following topics.

1. **Your Delight Song.** Using "The Delight Song of Tsoai-Talee" as a model, write your own delight song or poem. Use the following steps to help you.

   • Choose your favorite ideas, images, and feelings from the word map you made on page 197.
   • If you like, make metaphors from the ideas, images, and feelings.
   • Use the ideas, images, feelings, and metaphors to write a delight song. Repeat words or phrases that express your main idea.

2. **A Group Delight Song.** Work in small groups. Compare the word maps you made on page 197. If you like, make metaphors from the ideas, images, and feelings. Think of words or phrases that express the group's idea about delight. Use the ideas, images, feelings, and metaphors to write a delight song.

3. **Definition of Delight.** Write a definition of *delight*. First, explain what delight means to you. Then give examples of delight from your experience.

Peer Response

Work with a partner. Exchange papers and read each other's writing.* Discuss the following questions.

   • Does the writer use any strong images?
   • Does the writer use repetition?
   • What did you learn about the writer?
   • Do you have any questions for the writer?
   • What do you like best about the writing?

After you discuss your ideas, you may want to revise your writing. *(**Note:** If you wrote a group delight song, share your song with your classmates.)

About the Author

Born in Lawton, Oklahoma in 1934, N. Scott Momaday, a member of the Kiowa nation, grew up on various reservations where he attended Indian schools. He received a Ph.D. in Literature from Stanford University, where he became a professor of English and Comparative Literature. He is currently Regents Professor of English and Comparative Literature at the University of Arizona. His novel, *House Made of Dawn*, won the Pulitzer Prize for Fiction in 1969. "The Delight Song of Tsoai-Talee" is from his collection *Angle of Geese and Other Poems*. He is also the author of *The Way to Rainy Mountain*, the story of the migration of the Kiowa people from northern Montana to the southern Plains.

ON FURTHER REFLECTION

Making Connections

Discuss the following topics.

1. What is the mood of each piece of writing? Write an adjective describing it.

    "Just Lather, That's All" _____

    "Nearing 90" _____

    "Immortality" _____

    "The Delight Song of Tsoai-Talee" _____

2. Which character in the unit affected you most? Explain.
3. How do you think each writer feels about life and death? Explain.

Connecting to the Community

Choose one of the following projects.

1. Find out if you can visit a nursing home or other facility for elderly people in your community. Look in your local telephone book to see what facilities are available. Volunteer to read to or to participate in some other activity or program with one or more elderly persons. Report your experience to the class.
2. Invite an older person to speak to your class. Ask him or her how life has changed since his or her childhood.
3. A "life-or-death" issue is a topic that people consider very serious and important (for example, protecting the environment, helping political prisoners). What do you consider a life-or-death issue? Is there a local, national, or international organization that addresses this issue? Look in the phone book or check the Internet. Find out if there is an organization that needs volunteers. If so, ask what the volunteers do and how you can help. Report your findings to the class.

Answer Key

Note: Literary interpretation is often subjective, so answers will vary for many questions. Accordingly, while suggested answers are given, other answers are possible.

UNIT 1: FOOD

"Good Hot Dogs" by Sandra Cisneros

Comprehension
1. hot dog, French fries, and soda pop **2.** yellow mustard, onions **3.** Answers may vary. They probably were about 8-12 years old. **4.** <u>we'd run</u>, <u>humming</u>, <u>swinging my legs</u>

Focus on Reading: Visualizing
Possible strong pictures include: hot dogs in buns with yellow mustard and onions; French fries piled up; quarters on the counter, little burnt tips of the French fries

Focus on Literature: Poetic License
1. incomplete and run-on sentences; no punctuation marks **2.** Answers may vary. The short, incomplete sentences make the poem read very quickly, emphasizing how excited and hungry the poet and her friend were to eat the good hot dogs. **3.** Answers will vary.

Focus on Literature: Alliteration
The *–s* sound in *"smelled like steam"* (line 8); the *–h* sound in *"hold hot / in our hands"* (lines 20-21); the hard *–c* consonant sound in *"Quarters on the counter"* (line 23)

"The Way of Iced Coffee" by Donald W. George

Vocabulary
1. d **2.** j **3.** b **4.** c **5.** i **6.** e **7.** a **8.** f **9.** g **10.** h

Comprehension
1. He was sitting in a coffee shop in Tokyo, drinking iced coffee and watching people. **2.** He was feeling happy and relaxed. He was participating in a popular food ritual that made him feel part of the country and culture. **3.** He realized that his participation in the practice of drinking iced coffee was related to his sense of well being. **4.** It is a ritual because there is a particular way that people in Japanese coffee shops prepare and enjoy iced coffee. **5.** Answers will vary.

Focus on Reading: Sequence Words
4, 1, 6, 3, 5, 2

Focus on Literature: Similes
1. syrupy stream / a tiny waterfall **2.** syrupy stream / the dream of a rain shower on a summer afternoon **3.** cream-colored swirls and whirls and streams / a frozen breeze. **4.** ice cubes clinking / wind chimes in a seaside breeze.

"Food" by Victor M. Valle

Comprehension

1. Answers may vary. The poet may be suggesting that these observations are true for anyone. 2. *One* and *you* refer to "anyone" or "people in general." 3. The simple present can be used to show universal truths, which don't change over time. The simple past shows completed action or experience in the past. The poet suggests that these observations are true for all time.

Focus on Literature: Metaphors

Possible answers include:

A. *frijoles, earth* = brown;   *chile, sun and fire* = hot, fiery;   *water, sky* = refreshing

"The All-American Slurp" by Lensey Namioka

Vocabulary

1. c   2. b   3. e   4. h   5. a   6. j   7. d   8. f   9. g   10. i

Comprehension

1. They pulled strings out of their celery stalks and sat down at the buffet table. They felt mortified, embarrassed. 2. They ordered four dinners at random, not knowing what the food was. They slurped their soup. She was very embarrassed. 3. Meg put a lot of food on her plate and took more food before she finished what was on her plate. Mrs. Gleason mixed all the food together on her plate. Mr. Gleason couldn't use chopsticks well, so he picked up a pea with his fingers. 4. Answers will vary.

Focus on Reading: Guessing Meaning from Context

Answers may vary. Possible answers are: 2. *buffet dinner:* a dinner where people serve themselves food and then eat it in another room 3. *get acquainted with:* get to know; *kids:* children or young people 4. *promotion:* when a person gets a better or more important job 5. *stuffed:* very full, when you can't eat any more food

Focus on Literature: Onomatopoeia

1. *crunch, z-z-zip, shloop.* They all describe the sound of eating something.

UNIT 2: LOVE

"Oranges" by Gary Soto

Comprehension

1. Two oranges. Answers will vary. 2. Answers may vary. She wanted to look older, grown up, and perhaps more attractive to the boy. 3. To a drugstore. He wanted to buy her some candy. 4. Happy; *Light in her eyes, a smile / starting at the corners / Of her mouth.* 5. He gave the saleslady the nickel and one orange. Answers may vary. She knew he didn't have ten cents and didn't want to embarrass him in front of the girl. 6. He probably liked her because he smiled when he met

her, touched her shoulder, let her choose candy, and held her hand.   **7.** She probably liked him because she wore rouge, smiled and had light in her eyes when he asked her what she wanted, and let him hold her hand.   **8.** Answers may vary. Oranges may symbolize happiness in the poem. One orange helped the boy to pay for the candy when he didn't have enough money. The orange he peels at the end suggests brightness and warmth; perhaps this image shows how being with the girl made the boy feel.

Focus on Reading: Pronoun Referents

A.   1. She (line 13) = the girl;   **2.** we (line 20) = the boy and the girl   **3.** she (line 27) = the girl;   **4.** them (line 37) = the nickel and the orange;   **5.** them (line 40) = the saleslady's eyes;   **6.** it (line 49) = her hand.

B. They both understand that he is paying her with an orange because he doesn't have enough money to buy the candy.

Focus on Literature: Sensory Images

A. Answers may vary. Some possible answers include: **See:** My breath before me, then gone; Porch light burned yellow;   Face bright with rouge;   Candies tiered like bleachers;   Light in her eyes;   Fog hanging like old coats between the trees;   It was so bright against the gray of December   **Hear:** Frost cracking;   A dog barked;   The tiny bell bringing a saleslady;   A few cars hissing past; Unwrap the chocolate   **Touch/Feel:** Weighed down;   Touched her shoulder, and led her down the street;   I fingered a nickel;   The lady's eyes met mine and held them;   Fog hanging like old coats;   I took my girl's hand in mine for two blocks;   I peeled my orange;   A fire in my hands   **Smell:** Unwrap the chocolate;   I peeled my orange

B.   1. *Fog* is compared to *old coats*. The simile makes you see the darkish color and feel the thickness of the fog.   **2.** The "frost cracking" and "my breath / Before me, then gone" show the cold. The girl's "face bright / With rouge" and the boy's orange "so bright against / The gray of December" show how gray and colorless the winter day was. "A few cars hissing past" shows that there was moisture—perhaps from snow, rain, or fog—on the road.   **3.** Answers may vary. The image of the bright orange contrasts with the colorless gray of the weather and winter day.

4. Answers may vary. The bright color of the orange contrasted with the gray of the winter day may have looked like a fire in the boy's hands. The image of "a fire" in his hands suggests heat and excitement, perhaps the way the boy was feeling because he was with a girl he liked and held her hand.

"I Date a Thai" by Harvey Price

Vocabulary

1. e   **2.** f   **3.** a   **4.** b   **5.** d   **6.** c

Comprehension

1. Answers will vary.   **2.** Answers may vary. He probably expected to go somewhere with her to drink or eat something.   **3.** Answers may vary. She probably didn't know what a western-type date was like, so she just wanted to meet and spend a little time with him without anyone else knowing.   **4.** Answers will vary.   **5.** Answers will vary.

Focus on Reading: Quoted and Reported Speech

A. 1. one example   **2.** seven examples   **3.** He used more reported speech. His purpose was to describe—or report on—the unusual experience of his Thai date, not the conversation.
B. Quoted speech (other answers may be possible):   **2.** "Are you going to bring anyone with you?" she asked.   **3.** "I'll come alone also," she said.   **4.** "Don't tell anyone you're meeting me," she told me.   **5.** "Did you tell / Have you told anyone about our meeting?" she immediately asked.

Focus on Literature: Verbal Irony

1. Answers may vary. It suggests a date where a boy and girl do something together, such as have dinner or go to a movie.   **2.** Answers will vary.   **3.** The author's use of "date" in the title is ironic because he really didn't "date" a Thai—they didn't do anything and the experience lasted only 20 minutes.

"Wind and River Romance" by John Agard

Comprehension

A. 1. F **2.** F **3.** F **4.** T **5.** T **6.** T **7.** T **8.** F **9.** T **10.** F
B. 1. The River   **2.** He promises her the moon and stars. He'll do anything to win her love.
3. She believes that the Sea is faithful and the Wind is not.   **4.** Answers will vary.   **5.** Answers will vary.

Focus on Literature: Personification

Wind: plays loverboy; can't be trusted; talks fresh; whispers sweetly; brings others joy; tickles others   **River:** is not fooled or tricked; is a big woman   **Sea:** is faithful

"Rain Music" by Longhang Nguyen

Vocabulary

1. f **2.** i **3.** b **4.** a **5.** e **6.** l **7.** k **8.** j **9.** h **10.** d **11.** g **12.** c

Comprehension

1. They are sisters.   **2.** She met him at Cal, where they took classes together. They're friends.
3. She met him at UCSF, where they are both going to medical school. They're friends.   **4.** Linh's family knows that Thanh is Vietnamese, like them. They probably don't know about David because he is not Vietnamese. Linh's parents probably wouldn't approve of Linh's going out with David.
5. She doesn't feel comfortable telling her parents, but she is comfortable telling her sister.
6. Thanh. He is Vietnamese, very smart, and is studying to be a doctor.   **7.** Thanh. He is Vietnamese and she wants to marry someone from her own background and culture.
8. Answers may vary. "Rain Music" is the piano piece David played for Linh. The last image in the story is of rain pouring down the windshield of the car. Rain is a metaphor for tears, which Linh cries when she thinks of David.

Focus on Reading: Making Inferences

A. 1. I **2.** S **3.** S **4.** I **5.** I **6.** S **7.** S **8.** I **9.** I **10.** I

B. Answers may vary. **1.** Linh probably believes it is important to marry someone from her own background and culture, someone her parents approve of, and someone who has a good job and money to support her and her family. **2.** The author probably feels that it is important to have strong feelings for the person you marry. **3.** Perhaps she can't understand because she is younger and she isn't in the situation that her sister is. She may have different beliefs about love than her sister does.

Focus on Literature: Similes and Metaphors

A. 1. hair / cool satin (S) **2. a.** Linh / red rose (M) **b.** the author / green thorn (M) **3.** eyes / pearl-black pools (S) Also possible: eyes / almonds (M) **4.** skin / light honey (M) **5.** lips / rosebud (M)

B. Two other similes: (1) In paragraph 2, the author compares Linh's beauty to "notes in a chord being played separately, finger by finger, harmonizing back and forth." (2) In paragraph 21, Linh compares David's hands and fingers playing the piano to "little Russian men dancing in their black fur hats." Two other metaphors: (1) In paragraph 2, the author compares Linh's cheeks to velvet. (2) In paragraph 12, she compares Linh's soprano voice to a flute.

UNIT 3: CLOTHES

"Ode to My Socks" by Pablo Neruda

Comprehension

A. 1. Maru Mori **2.** She made them (knitted them). **3.** Answers may vary. She's probably a friend. Giving the socks was a friendly gesture. **4.** Wonderful. We can infer this from his descriptions of the socks in the poem. **5.** Winter. He was especially grateful to have wool socks in the cold weather of winter.

B. Possible adjectives: violent, heavenly, handsome, glowing, magnificent, wool

Focus on Reading: A Moral

1. Answers may vary. He might mean that a gift is twice as beautiful and doubly good when it is both beautiful and useful. He might also be playing with the image of the two socks as two separate items—each sock was beautiful and would keep one of his feet warm.

Focus on Literature: An Ode

1. Answers will vary. He has very strong feelings about the socks. He says they are heavenly, handsome, and magnificent. **2.** Answers may vary. An ode is a song of praise so he is praising the socks and thinks they are a special gift. He feels honored to have them. **3.** The poet uses unusual and exaggerated language to describe a simple and common article of clothing, so the ode is funny.

Expansion

1. The poet compares the socks to rabbits. They are both very soft.   **2.** (1) two fish made of wool, (2) two long sharks, (3) two immense blackbirds, (4) two cannons.   **3.** Answers may vary. The poet resisted the temptation not to wear the socks. He was tempted not to wear the socks because they were so magnificent that he felt his feet seemed unworthy of them. But he resisted the temptation and wore them because he knew how good the socks would feel.

"Getups" by Maya Angelou

Vocabulary

1. e **2.** f **3.** g **4.** a **5.** j **6.** i **7.** c **8.** b **9.** d **10.** h

Comprehension

1. Answers will vary. Possible words: young, hard-working, creative, responsible, confident, sensitive   **2.** She bought clothes at second-hand shops because she was a single parent and didn't have a lot of money.   **3.** She felt very comfortable wearing her clothes and felt happy when she created her own fashion.   **4.** He felt embarrassed because she wore bright colors and unusual clothes, different from other mothers.   **5.** Answers will vary. Possible definition: strange or unusual clothes, created by mixing styles and colors   **6.** She feels it is important to buy clothes that look good on her, that make her feel good about herself, and that make her feel comfortable.

Focus on Reading: Making Inferences

1. Possible answer: "Mother, I'd like you to wear sweaters that match."   **2.** Possible answer: "Mother, please don't come to school unless they call you."   **3.** Possible answer: "That person isn't cool because he/she isn't wearing the latest fashion."

Focus on Literature: Thesis and Antithesis

1. c **2.** b **3.** <u>Thesis statements</u>: Seek the fashion which truly fits and befits you. You will always be in fashion if you are true to yourself, and only if you are true to yourself. Try rather to be so much yourself that the clothes you choose increase your naturalness and grace. <u>Antithesis statements</u>: The statement "Clothes make the man" should be looked at, reexamined, and in fact re-evaluated. Clothes can make the man or woman look silly and foppish and foolish.

"Girl with the Green Skirt" by Dana Naone

Comprehension

1. She walks down a road in a green skirt.   **2.** They try to attract her attention by taking off their shirts.   **3.** She probably notices them, but she ignores them. She keeps on walking.   **4.** They try harder to get her attention, by holding out their arms. She continues to ignore them.   **5.** They give up in frustration. They realize she isn't going to pay them any attention.

Focus on Literature: Figures of Speech

A. 1. skirt / surface of a pond; Answers will vary.   **2.** arms / branches of a tree; Answers will vary.   **3.** skirt / green forest; Answers will vary.   **4.** skirt / girl   **5.** *Crushed leaves* don't produce *water.* The oxymoron suggests that the men want something that they can't have: They can't squeeze water from leaves, and they can't get the girl's attention.   **6.** *Green* replaces *the girl.*

"The Red Coat" by John Patrick Shanley

Comprehension

1. He left the party because Mary wasn't there.   **2.** He suddenly told her that he loved her.   **3.** He's loved her for months, since the time they had a snowball fight.   **4.** He remembered Mary's red coat.   **5.** He liked the way Mary looked in the coat and he sensed something about it.   **6.** She's had the coat for many years and it reminds her of all the good things from her childhood. Wearing the red coat is like being grown up and having her childhood, like being safe in an adventure.   **7.** She's always wanted someone to understand how she feels about the red coat. It's very special to her and it links her adulthood and childhood.

Focus on Reading: Reduced Forms

2. Why did you leave the party because I wasn't there?   **3.** I don't know.   **4.** I shouldn't have said it.   **5.** Sometimes, in a movie the hero's doing all this stuff that's dangerous, but you know, because of the kind of movie it is, that he's not going to get hurt.   **6.** Being in the red coat is like that . . . like being safe in an adventure.

UNIT 4: GROWING UP

"When I Was Young on an Island" by Diane Kahanu

Comprehension

1. Stanza 1: catching and killing a shark; Stanza 2: catching an eel and feeding it to the cat; Stanza 3: the battle charge; Stanza 4: the jellyfish test   **2.** On an island, near the ocean. The children's activities were all related to the ocean.   **3.** The poet's brother, who was the leader and who organized the games.   **4.** She is his sister.

Focus on Reading: Making Inferences

1. She had a brother and played with him and other children. She really looked up to her brother because he was a leader and she and the other children followed him.   **2.** He liked to catch sharks and eels. He was a leader and the other children followed him. He liked to invent games that tested him and the other children.   **3.** She looked up to him because her poem is about the different activities he led. She always took part in the games he invented, even when it caused her pain. She probably did these things to prove herself to him.   **4.** Their lives were closely connected to the ocean and beach, and they usually played outside. Their play made use of objects and animals from the island, such as driftwood, sharks, eels, and jellyfish.

Focus on Literature: Literal and Figurative Meanings

1. L   **2.** L   **3.** F: bullets / sand, wind's hand   **4.** F: He / Apache Indian   **5.** L

"Why Boys Don't Know What Girls Mean and Girls Think Boys Are Mean" by Deborah Tannen

Vocabulary
A. 2. h **3.** e **4.** d **5.** g **6.** a **7.** b **8.** c **B. 2.** kids **3.** ruined **4.** consequences
5. shield **6.** insignificant **7.** amusing **8.** buddies

Comprehension
A. 1. Girls **2.** Boys **3.** Girls and Boys **4.** Boys **5.** Girls and Boys **6.** Boys **7.** Girls
8. Boys **9.** Girls **10.** Boys
B. 1. Girls say boys are mean. Boys say that it's hard to know what girls really mean. **2.** She believes these attitudes come from differences in the way girls and boys learn to play with their friends as children. **3.** He observed that the two boys and one girl didn't have the same idea of what was fun. The boys liked destroying each other's creations, but the girl didn't. **4.** They observed that (1) the girls negotiated their friendships and rivalries privately, but boys did this publicly; (2) the boys and girls reacted differently when their friends showed their feelings; and (3) the girls did not like strangers overhearing their conversation, but the boys liked it. **5.** Since boys and girls have different ideas of how to do things together and how to talk about what they want, it can be dangerous for girls if boys want to do something the girls do not want to do. **6.** Once girls understand the different ways that boys and girls interact, they should concentrate on what they want and don't want and make this clear to boys.

Focus on Reading: Guessing Meaning from Context
2. deny: hide **3. gathering:** a group of people meeting together, such as a birthday party
4. insulted: said something to make someone feel bad **5. in charge:** responsible for someone or something **6. share:** have the same idea about something **7. gender:** sex; male or female

Focus on Literature: Theme and Thesis
1. Boys and girls have different attitudes about each other. **2.** (Boys and girls) have different ideas of how to do things together and how to talk about what they want. **3.** The thesis suggests that the author will include information about boys' and girls' attitudes and behavior. **4.** It suggests that part of the essay will describe boys' attitudes and behavior, and the other part will describe girls' attitudes and behavior.

"Abuela Invents the Zero" by Judith Ortiz Cofer

Vocabulary
A. 1. e **2.** g **3.** f **4.** h **5.** a **6.** j **7.** i **8.** b **9.** c **10.** d **B. 1.** compromise
2. packed **3.** shrinking **4.** lame **5.** jerk **6.** hands over **7.** retrieve **8.** means business
9. support **10.** cringe

Comprehension
1. She wanted to see snow and visit her daughter and her family. **2.** She wears her daughter's coat, which is too big for her. Constancia is embarrassed and doesn't want to be seen with her.

3. He won't let her have the car to meet her friends if she doesn't promise to take Abuela to church.   **4.** The grandmother gets lost. Constancia feels embarrassed.   **5.** She ignores her grandmother. Her grandmother feels angry and upset.   **6.** Her grandmother tells Constancia's parents that she made her feel like a zero. When her mother finds out what happened in the church, she sends Constancia to her room.   **7.** She feels like a jerk and is sorry.

Focus on Reading: Distinguishing Fact from Opinion
A. 1. F **2.** F **3.** O **4.** O **5.** F **6.** O **7.** O **8.** O **9.** F **10.** F **11.** O
12. F

"Blue Stone" by Richard Hugo

Vocabulary
1. b 2. a 3. c 4. a 5. b 6. b

Comprehension
1. It comes from a big blue stone no one can find.   **2.** It can veer your life away from poverty to riches. It can grow a tree exactly where you need shade.   **3.** He acts indifferent and nonchalant. They work better for him when he acts that way.   **4.** Armies start marching.   **5.** Armies stop marching.   **6.** He knows they've returned to the big blue stone somewhere in the blue mountains.

Focus on Reading: Visualizing
A. Possible images: huge blue stone, speck of sky, tiny bit of sea, blue marble shooter, long blue day, bird sings blue rain, blue mountains
B. 1. Most of the images are of nature or the natural world.
2. They might suggest that the poet feels the blue stone, like all of nature, is magical and mysterious.   **3.** He probably feels a sense of wonder toward nature because of the way he describes it and the stone.

UNIT 5: WORK

"Jorge the Church Janitor Finally Quits" by Martín Espada

Comprehension
1. He is probably from Honduras, since he mentions this country in the poem.   **2.** Spanish. He probably doesn't speak English well. He works as a janitor, a job that requires few language skills. If he spoke English well he might have communicated better with the people at his job.   **3.** Perhaps the people don't care. Perhaps they assume Jorge doesn't understand English.   **4.** Jorge probably means that no one can pronounce his Spanish name correctly.   **5.** Answers will vary.
6. Answers may vary. He feels angry and/or unimportant.   **7.** *Finally* means "after a long time." This suggests that he is quitting after a long time of being unhappy.   **8.** Second stanza: toilet/punchbowl; fourth stanza: mop/squid. Answers will vary.

Focus on Reading: Pronoun Referents

A. 1. no one (line 1) = none of the people at the church where Jorge works   **2.** their (line 8) = the people who see him working   **3.** they (line 19) = people who have spoken to Jorge or have observed his behavior   **4.** they (line 30) = the people at the church who find the mop after Jorge has quit   **5.** it (line 30) = the mop

B. Answers may vary. By using *no one*, *their* and *they*, the poet emphasizes that Jorge is talking about all the people he had contact with at work. This suggests that he did not have any personal relationships with people at work, that perhaps no one bothered to get to know him.

Focus on Literature: Dramatic Monologue

1. It makes the poem more direct and intense, like a real person is speaking to the reader. He has something important to tell the reader: that he just quit his job.   **2.** It reveals that he is probably intelligent but that he is also angry.   **3.** It reveals that he is angry and unhappy about his job and the people he worked for.   **4.** Answers may vary. The poet probably feels sympathetic toward Jorge because he makes Jorge the speaker of the poem so that Jorge can communicate his feelings directly to the reader.   **5.** Answers may vary. He probably wants the reader to feel and understand the anger and frustration of some people in menial jobs because often no one pays attention to them.

"Bottleman" by Eric Bogosian

Vocabulary
1. d **2.** e **3.** a **4.** f **5.** b **6.** c

Comprehension
1. A pack of cigarettes, an egg salad sandwich, a cup of coffee, a newspaper, and a place to sit down. **2.** Cigarettes are easy to get. An egg salad sandwich is difficult to get.   **3.** From newspapers that he finds.   **4.** Hotels are too expensive. He might sleep in the doorways of buildings or on the ground in the park.   **5.** Wood is softer and more comfortable than concrete.   **6.** Answers may vary. "I stay on the sunny side of the street" means "I try to look at life in a positive way." "Half a glass of water is better than no water" means "Something is better than nothing." "The early bird catches the worm" means "The person who gets up early and starts work will be successful." The sayings show how Bottleman tries to make the best out of his difficult life, and to be successful in his own way.

Focus on Reading: Reduced Forms
2. Who's going to take care of me?   **3.** I want to know about the world.   **4.** Who's got that kind of money?   **5.** They used to make benches out of wood.

"A Letter to God" by Gregorio López y Fuentes

Vocabulary
1. d **2.** j **3.** g **4.** h **5.** a **6.** e **7.** i **8.** c **9.** f **10.** b

Comprehension

1. The farm is on the crest of a hill, overlooking a river. His land is dry and it needs rain.   **2.** He predicts rain. His prediction comes true—it rains—but then the rain turns to hail.   **3.** The raindrops are like coins because they make his crops grow so he can sell them and make money.   **4.** Lencho is probably a big, strong man who works very hard, like an ox.   **5.** He needs help to plant new crops and feed his family. He asks for 100 pesos.   **6.** He opens the letter, and then collects 70 pesos to send to Lencho. He admires Lencho's faith and doesn't want him to lose that faith.   **7.** He feels like he was cheated. He thinks God sent him 100 pesos but the post-office employees stole 30.   **8.** He writes a second letter. He asks God to send 30 more pesos but not to send it through the mail because he still doesn't know the truth.

Focus on Literature: Dramatic Irony

1. He thinks the post-office employees stole it.   **2.** The post-office employees really gave Lencho the 70 pesos; they didn't have 100 pesos.   **3.** At the very end, when Lencho writes his second letter.   **4.** Yes. The reader knows the truth about the money, but Lencho doesn't.   **5.** Answers may vary. The author's use of dramatic irony probably surprises and amuses most readers.

Focus on Reading: Inferring a Moral

1. Lencho asks God for more money.   **2.** The contrast between what Lencho *thinks* has happened and what the reader *knows* has really happened.   **3.** Answers may vary. One possible lesson is that ordinary people are capable of unexpected and secret acts of kindness. Another possible lesson is that people should not be so quick to judge other people.   **4.** Answers may vary. The ironic ending is more powerful because the reader isn't expecting it.

"Follow Your Passion" by Johnnetta B. Cole

Vocabulary

1. g   **2.** h   **3.** e   **4.** a   **5.** k   **6.** j   **7.** c   **8.** i   **9.** b   **10.** d   **11.** l   **12.** f

Comprehension

1. A pediatrician. She didn't want to work for her father; she knew being a doctor impressed grown-ups; at the time, pediatrics was seen as appropriate for women; and she liked babies.
2. At Fisk University, where she took an anthropology class with Professor Simpson.   **3.** She was interested in the connections among different kinds of people.   **4.** Her grandfather. He implied that she would never be able to make a living as an anthropologist.   **5.** She told her to follow her passion because if she did something she hated, she would be unhappy.   **6.** She thinks it was among the best advice she ever received. She is passing the advice on in her essay.   **7.** Her choice to be an anthropologist has brought her great joy and satisfaction.   **8.** She advises them to follow their passion.

Focus on Reading: Theme

1. Answers may vary. People should do work that they really care about.   **2.** If this is your passion, then follow it (paragraph 11). Always my answer was the same: "Follow your passion"

(paragraph 21).   **3.** She states it directly, even in the title of the essay. She wants her theme to be completely clear.   **4.** Answers may vary. The quote suggests that if you don't follow your passion and do work you really care about, you will be miserable.

Focus on Literature: Motif

1. Follow your passion. The exact words appear twice: in the title and in paragraph 21. However, the same idea/motif is paraphrased in paragraphs 11, 24, and 25.   **2.** Answers may vary. It is simple, direct, and easy to remember. Also, it was advice from her mother.   **3.** Answers will vary.

UNIT 6: LIFE AND DEATH

"Just Lather, That's All" by Hernando Téllez

Vocabulary

A. 1. e **2.** h **3.** i **4.** f **5.** a **6.** d **7.** b **8.** j **9.** g **10.** c
B. 1. rebels **2.** expedition **3.** slit **4.** client **5.** conceal **6.** taking pains **7.** faction
8. executioner **9.** tender **10.** services

Comprehension

1. The barber and the captain. Answers will vary: The barber is nervous, thoughtful, conscientious. The captain is confident, strict, ruthless.   **2.** He starts to tremble. The captain is in charge of the government troops, and the barber is a rebel.   **3.** He says that he caught fourteen rebels. The barber is upset.   **4.** He implies that he will execute all the rebels. The barber's hands start trembling again.   **5.** He takes his job seriously, is proud of it, and is careful and conscientious.
6. Even though he is a rebel, the barber doesn't believe it is right to murder another person.
7. The captain tells the barber that he wanted to find out if the barber would kill him. Answers may vary: Readers are probably surprised because they don't know that the captain knows the barber is a rebel.

Focus on Literature: Conflict

1. The external conflict is the war between the government troops and the rebels. The internal conflict is between the barber and the captain: The barber must choose whether or not to kill the captain, and the captain knows the barber is a rebel but wants to see if the barber will kill him.
2. Both. It is external (the revolution) and internal (in the minds of the two main characters).
3. The barber's. He probably did this to allow him to build tension and create his surprise ending.
4. Answers may vary. The barber realizes he won't kill the captain. He wants only lather on his hands (because he is a barber, and lather is part of the job), not blood (because he is not a murderer).

"Nearing 90" by William Maxwell

Vocabulary

1. g **2.** f **3.** i **4.** h **5.** e **6.** b **7.** a **8.** c **9.** j **10.** d

Comprehension

1. He was eighty-eight and a half.   **2.** He wants to reread every book that he has ever deeply enjoyed.   **3.** Answers may vary: He knows that he has already lived a long time and that death is inevitable.   **4.** He remembers sleigh riding with his parents and taking a riverboat ride with his parents. He remembers the happy feeling of the sleigh ride and the scary fact that the riverboat later sank, killing many people.   **5.** He remembers carrying them on his shoulders, reading to them, and studying their faces. His children were special to him then and are special to him now that he is old.   **6.** Answers will vary.

Focus on Reading: Phrasal Verbs

1. d **2.** i **3.** b **4.** e **5.** h **6.** c **7.** j **8.** a **9.** g **10.** f

Focus on Literature: Flashbacks

1. It relates to his thoughts about his poor posture: His father used to tell him to stand up straight.   **2.** He compares roses, children, and the very old—and indicates that all three things reflect their care.   **3.** It has helped him to accept the inevitability of his own death and to not be afraid of death.   **4.** The sleigh ride with his parents. It indicates that he felt safe and happy with his parents.   **5.** His ride on the riverboat Eastland and then learning that the boat had sunk a year later. He feels like he had escaped death because he had been on the boat a year before.   **6.** It shows that the author is a parent. His children were—and are—special to him.

"Immortality" by Maria Testa

Vocabulary

1. b **2.** d **3.** h **4.** f **5.** e **6.** a **7.** g **8.** c

Comprehension

1. Fourteen. **2.** Younger. **3.** Sandra, the author's sister. She was at least sixteen. **4.** They were racing in a car against two boys in another car. It was the narrator's idea. **5.** Two boys, Mikey and Tony. They are friends. **6.** The boys' car. The girls were slowing down to get off the highway, but the boys were still driving fast on the highway. Perhaps the police didn't see the girls' car; or, if they did see it, they wanted to catch the boys who were still driving fast. **7.** In the parking lot of the China Inn restaurant. They planned to meet the boys and eat Chinese food. **8.** Tina probably felt afraid and angry. She realized they could have had an accident and been killed. **9.** Because the narrator had suggested the idea of racing the boys.

Focus on Literature: Mood

1. Answers may vary. Possible adjectives: tense, afraid, excited, scared **2.** Answers may vary. Possible images: screaming her head off; slapped both hands against the dashboard; swore in Italian; swerved neatly across two lanes; shot past; speeding our brains out; whipped past

Focus on Literature: Register

1. Informal. She uses a lot of slang and her language is very conversational. **2.** Teenagers use informal register when talking to each other, so the author wants her characters to sound natural and real.

"The Delight Song of Tsoai-Talee" by N. Scott Momaday

Comprehension

1. The first part has a narrower focus because the poet names or lists specific things. The second part has a broader focus because it relates more general aspects of the poet's life.   **2.** The pronoun *I*. He might be talking to himself, as if in a kind of prayer. Or he might be addressing the reader.   **3.** He uses the pronoun *You* in addition to *I*. He might be addressing the reader, or perhaps *Tsen-tainte* (White Horse), or perhaps also the daughter of *Tsen-tainte*.   **4.** He repeats the verbs *am* (a form of *be*) and *stand*. In the context of the poem, *stand* means *exist* or *be*. By repeating *am* and *stand*, the poet emphasizes *being* or *existing* in harmony with nature, people, and his life.

Focus on Literature: List Poem

1. Most of the items are elements or aspects of nature.   **2.** They are part of nature, the natural world.   **3.** Answers may vary. The poet honors and respects nature. He sees himself as part of nature, and in balance and harmony with nature.

Focus on Literature: Chant

1. *I am . . .*   **2.** *You see, I am; I stand in good relation to . . .*   **3.** Answers will vary.   **4.** Answers may vary. He probably wants to express his feeling of delight and harmony with nature. **5.** Answers may vary. By repeating *I am* and *I stand*, the poet emphasizes his existing in harmony with nature.

Expansion

A. Answers may vary. Some possible answers include: **Earth:** *shadow that follows a child; deer standing away in the dusk; a field of sumac*   **Air:** *eagle playing in the wind; the farthest star; angle of geese in the winter sky*   **Fire:** *the evening light, the lustre of meadows; a flame of four colors*   **Water:** *fish in the water; the roaring of the rain*

B. 1. Answers will vary.   **2.** He feels delight and wonder toward all of nature and life.   **3.** Answers may vary. He probably uses his Kiowa name because he is part of the Kiowa people and his feelings toward nature and life reflect those of his people. Perhaps he is in love with Tsen-tainte's daughter and his feelings toward her are connected to his feelings toward all of nature and life.

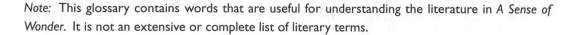

Glossary of Literary Terms

Note: This glossary contains words that are useful for understanding the literature in *A Sense of Wonder.* It is not an extensive or complete list of literary terms.

Alliteration the use of words that begin with the same consonant sound at the beginning of words in order to create rhythm or other special effects, especially in poetry

Antithesis the exact opposite of something, or something that is completely different from something else; a counter-argument (Compare: **Thesis**)

Backstory a short biography or personal history that an actor creates for a character, which helps the actor understand and play the character

Chant words or phrases that are repeated again and again; a form of poetry in which one or more lines are repeated again and again

Characterization the way in which a writer makes a person in a story, movie, or play seem like a real person

Conflict a struggle between one or more characters in a story

Dramatic Irony a way of giving information in a story in which the reader knows something that the characters do not, and can understand the real importance of what is happening

Dramatic Monologue a poem or other form of writing in which one character speaks directly to the reader

Fantasy an idea or situation that is created by the imagination and which could not happen in real life; writing that includes unreal or magical characters, situations or events

Figurative Meaning the meaning of a word or expression that is different from the usual one, to give you a picture in your mind (Compare: **Literal Meaning**)

Figure of Speech the meaning of a word or expression that is different from the usual meanings of the words, in order to give you a picture in your mind; four common figures of speech are similes, metaphors, metonyms, and oxymorons

Flashback a scene in a story, movie, play, essay, etc. that shows something that happened before that point in the story

Hyperbole a way of describing something by saying it is much bigger, smaller, better, worse, etc. than it really is; exaggeration, usually for humorous effect

List Poem a poem in which the poet gives a list of items—people, places, things, events, experiences, ideas—that are similar or related in some way and which have special meaning to the poet

Literal Meaning the usual meaning of a word or expression (Compare: **Figurative Meaning**)

Metaphor a way of describing something by comparing it to something else without using the words *like* or *as* (Compare: **Simile**)

Metonym a word or expression that replaces the name of one thing with the name of something else related to it

Mood the way that a piece of literature makes you feel

Motif a phrase, idea, or image that is repeated or developed in a piece of literature

Ode a poem or song that is written to praise a person or thing

Onomatopoeia the use of words that sound like the action or thing they are describing

Oxymoron an expression that combines two opposite or contrasting ideas

Personification the representation of a thing or quality as a person

Poetic License the freedom of writers—especially poets—to break traditional grammar and punctuation rules in order to express ideas and feelings

Register the way a writer or speaker uses language in a particular social context

Sensory Image an image that describes the way something looks, feels, tastes, sounds, or smells

Simile an expression that describes something by comparing it to something else, using the words *like* or *as*; writers use similes to create strong images (Compare: **Metaphor**)

Theme a main subject or idea in a piece of writing, speech, movie, etc.; the general idea or subject of an essay

Thesis a writer's main idea, opinion, or argument in an essay (Compare: **Antithesis**)

Verbal Irony the use of words to say the opposite of what you mean